YOUR **TOTAL SOLUTION** FOR **Second Grade**

Carson-Dellosa Publishing LLC
P.O. Box 35665 • Greensboro, NC 27425 USA

carsondellosa.com

Carson-Dellosa Publishing, LLC
PO Box 35665
Greensboro, NC 27425 USA
carsondellosa.com

ISBN 978-1-4838-1295-3

01-335141151

Table of Contents

Welcome to *Your Total Solution for Second Grade*!

Building a strong foundation is an essential part of your child's success. *Your Total Solution* features a variety of activity pages that make learning fun, keeping your child engaged and entertained at the same time. Designed by experts in elementary education, these workbooks will help children meet important proficiency standards with activities that strengthen their math and reading skills. Each book is structured to give your child an advantage in the classroom and beyond!

Your Total Solution for Second Grade is designed for learning reinforcement and can be used as a tool for independent study. This comprehensive workbook includes:

- Practice in basic reading concepts, skills, and strategies.
- Drill and practice in essential math concepts.
- Lessons that encourage critical thinking.
- A thorough presentation and practice of skills used on standardized tests.
- A complete answer key to support independent learning.

This book provides an outstanding educational experience and important learning tools to prepare your child for the future. *Your Total Solution for Second Grade* offers hours of educational entertainment that will make your child want to come back for more!

READING

Name _____

Beginning Consonants: b, c, d, f, g, h, j

Directions: Fill in the beginning consonant for each word.

Example: __c__ at

__b__ ox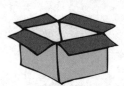

__J__ acket

__g__ oat

__h__ ouse

__d__ og

__f__ ire

Your Total Solution for Second Grade

Name _____

Beginning Consonants: k, l, m, n, p, q, r

Directions: Write the letter that makes the beginning sound for each picture.

r   P   b   L

M   L   k   r

qu   P   n   m

ʯ   k   r   w

Name _____

Beginning Consonants: s, t, v, w, x, y, z

Directions: Write the letter under each picture that makes the beginning sound.

© Carson-Dellosa • CD-704644   Your Total Solution for Second Grade

Ending Consonants: b, d, f, g

Directions: Fill in the ending consonant for each word.

ma d _____

cu b _____

roo f _____

do _g_____

be d _____

bi g _____

Name _____

Ending Consonants: k, l, m, n, p, r

Directions: Fill in the ending consonant for each word.

nai _l_

ca _n_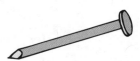

gu _k_

ca _r_

truc _k_

ca _p_

pai _l_

Your Total Solution for Second Grade

Ending Consonants: s, t, x

Directions: Fill in the ending consonant for each word.

ca _t_

bo _x_

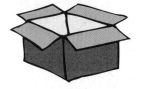

bu _ss_

fo _x_

boa _t_

ma _t_

Name _____

Consonant Blends

Consonant blends are two or three consonant letters in a word whose sounds combine, or blend. **Examples: br, fr, gr, pr, tr**

Directions: Look at each picture. Say its name. Write the blend you hear at the beginning of each word.

tree

frog

brom

presnt

trck

grap

dic

glass

brosh

tringle

wig

trash

Your Total Solution for Second Grade

Consonant Blends: bl, sl, cr, cl

Directions: Look at the pictures and say their names. Write the letters for the beginning sound in each word.

<u>cl</u>own

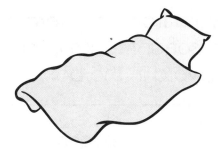

<u>bl</u>anket

<u>cr</u>ayon

<u>cl</u>ock

<u>sl</u>ide

<u>cl</u>oud

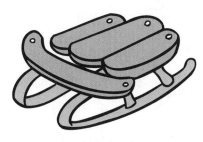

<u>sl</u>ed

<u>cr</u>ab

<u>cr</u>ocodile

Name _____

Consonant Teams

Consonant teams are two or three consonant letters that have a single sound. **Examples: sh** and **tch**

Directions: Write each word from the word box next to its picture. Underline the consonant team in each word. Circle the consonant team in each word in the box.

bench	match	shoe	thimble
shell	brush	peach	watch
whale	teeth	chair	wheel

 shoe   thimble

 wheel   watch

 chair   peach

 whale   match

 bench   shell

 brush   teeth

Your Total Solution for Second Grade

Consonant Teams

Directions: Read the words in the box. Write a word from the word box to finish each sentence. Circle the consonant team in each word. **Hint:** There are three letters in each team!

splash	screen	spray	street	scream
screw	shrub	split	strong	string

1. Another word for a bush is a Shrub_____.

2. I tied a String_____ to my tooth to help pull it out.

3. I have many friends who live on my street_____.

4. We always scream_____ when we ride the roller coaster.

5. A Screen_____ helps keep bugs out of the house.

6. It is fun to _____Splash_____ in the water.

7. My father uses an ax to split_____ the firewood.

8. We will need a ___Screw_____ to fix the chair.

9. You must be very _____Strong_____ to lift this heavy box.

10. The firemen _____Spray_____ the fire with the water.

Name _____

Letter Teams: sh, ch, wh, th

Directions: Look at the first picture in each row. Circle the pictures that have the same sound.

whistle

shoe

chin

thumb

Your Total Solution for Second Grade

Short Vowels

Vowels can make **short** or **long** sounds. The short **a** sounds like the **a** in **cat**. The short **e** is like the **e** in **leg**. The short **i** sounds like the **i** in **pig**. The short **o** sounds like the **o** in **box**. The short **u** sounds like the **u** in **cup**.

Directions: Look at each picture. Write the missing short vowel letter.

p _u_ p   n _e_ t   s _o_ ck

_o_ x   l _i_ ps   h _a_ t

f _o_ x   t _e_ nt   p _i_ n

Name _____

Short Vowels

Directions: Look at the pictures. Their names all have short vowel sounds. But the vowels are missing! Fill the missing vowels in each word.

a, e, i, o, u

p_u_pp_e_t

h_a_mmer

p_o_pcorn

_e_l_e_ph_a_nt

t_e_l_e_v_i_sion

b_o_ttle

sh_o_v_e_l

th_u_mble

c_a_ndle

b_u_tt_o_n

p_e_nny

l_a_dder

Your Total Solution for Second Grade

Short a Words

Directions: Use a word from the box to complete each sentence.

fat	path	lamp	can
van	stamp	Dan	math
sat	cat	fan	bat

Example:

1. The __lamp__ had a pink shade.

2. The bike _path_ led us to the park.

3. I like to add in _math_ class.

4. The cat is very _fat_ .

5. The _can_ of beans was hard to open.

6. The envelope needed a _stamp_ .

7. He swung the _bat_ and hit the ball.

8. The _fan_ blew air around.

9. My mom drives a blue _van_ .

10. I _sat_ in the backseat.

Name _____

Short e Words

Directions: Say each word and listen for the short **e** sound. Then, write each word and underline the letter that makes the short **e** sound.

1 get	2 Meg	3 rest	4 tent
5 red	6 spent	7 test	8 help
9 bed	10 pet	11 head	12 best

1. get _____

2. Meg _____

3. rest _____

4. tent _____

5. red _____

6. spent _____

7. test _____

8. help _____

9. bead _____

10. pet _____

11. head _____

12. best _____

Your Total Solution for Second Grade

Short i Words

Directions: Complete the sentences by matching the words to the correct sentence.

1. I made a _wish_ on a star.

2. All we could see was the shark's _fin_ above the water.

3. I like to eat vegetables with _fish_ .

4. We saw lots of _____ in the water.

5. The soccer player will _____ the ball and score a goal.

6. If you feel _Sick_, see a doctor.

7. Did Bob _____ the race?

8. The _____ was full of candy.

fin

fish

kick

win

dish

dip

wish

sick

Name _____

Short o Words

Directions: Use the short **o** words in the box to write rhyming words.

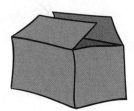

hot	rock	lock	cot
stop	sock	fox	mop
box	mob	clock	Bob

1. Write the words that rhyme with **dot**.

cot   _hot_

2. Write the words that rhyme with **socks**.

fox   _lock_

3. Write the words that rhyme with **hop**.

mop   _Sock_

4. Write the words that rhyme with **dock**.

rock   _lock_

5. Write the words that rhyme with **cob**.

Mob   _Bob_

Your Total Solution for Second Grade

Short u Words

Directions: Say each word and listen for the short **u** sound. Then, write each word and underline the letter that makes the short **u** sound.

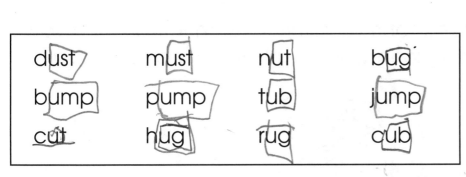

dust	must	nut	bug
bump	pump	tub	jump
cut	hug	rug	cub

1. Cut

2. hug

3. bug

4. dust

5. must

6. rug

7. cub

8. tub

9. nut

10. bump

11. pump

12. jump

Name _____

Long Vowels

Long vowel sounds have the same sound as their names. When a **Super Silent e** comes at the end of a word, you can't hear it, but it changes the vowel sound to a long vowel sound.

Example: rope, skate, bee, pie, cute

Directions: Say the name of the pictures. Listen for the long vowel sounds. Write the missing long vowel sound under each picture.

c __a__ ke   h __i__ ke   n __o__ se

__a__ pe   c __u__ be   gr __a__ pe

r __a__ ke   b __o__ ne   k __i__ te

Your Total Solution for Second Grade

Long a Words

Directions: Write the words in order so that each sentence tells a complete idea. Begin each sentence with a capital letter and end it with a period or a question mark.

1. plate was on the cake a

A plate was on the cake.

2. like you would to play a game

Do you would to play a games?

3. gray around the a corner train came

There is gray around the a corner train came

4. was on mail Bob's name the

There's was on mail Bob's name.

5. sail for on day we went a nice a

There for a sail on day we went for nice boat trip

Name _____

Long e Words

Long **e** is the vowel sound which says its own name. Long **e** can be spelled **ee** as in the word **teeth**, **ea** as in the word **meat**, or **e** as in the word **me**.

Directions: Say each word and listen for the long **e** sound. Then, write the words and underline the letters that make the long **e** sound.

street	neat	treat	feet
sleep	keep	deal	meal
mean	clean	beast	feast

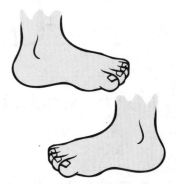

1. _deep_

2. _mean_

3. _clean_

4. _beast_

5. _neat_

6. _street_

7. _feet_

8. _sleep_

9. _treat_

10. _deal_

11. _meal_

12. _feast_

Your Total Solution for Second Grade

Long i Words

Long **i** is the sound you hear in the word **fight**.

Directions: Use the long **i** words in the box to write rhyming words.

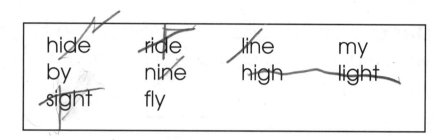

hide	ride	line	my
by	nine	high	light
sight	fly		

1. Write the words that rhyme with **sigh**.

high _hidett_ ____ _high_

2. Write the words that rhyme with **side**.

ride _line_ _nine_

3. Write the words that rhyme with **fine**.

line _ride_ _hide_

4. Write the words that rhyme with **fight**.

sight _light_

Name _____Siri_____

Long o Words

Long **o** is the vowel sound which says its own name. Long **o** can be spelled **oa** as in the word **float** or **o** with a silent **e** at the end as in **cone**.

Directions: Say each word and listen for the long **o** sound. Then, write each word and underline the letters that make the long **o** sound.

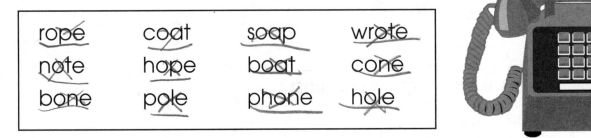

rope	coat	soap	wrote
note	hope	boat	cone
bone	pole	phone	hole

1. rope.

2. Note.

3. bone.

4. coat.

5. hope.

6. pole.

7. Soap.

8. boat.

9. phone.

10. wrote.

11. cone

12. hol

Your Total Solution for Second Grade

Long u Words

Directions: Write the words in the sentences below in the correct order. Begin each sentence with a capital letter and end it with a period or a question mark.

1. the pulled dentist tooth my loose

_The dentist pulled My tooth.___

2. ice cubes I choose in my drink to put

_I choose MY ice Cubes in my to___
_pushin in my za.___

3. a Ruth fuse blew yesterday

_____

_____

4. loose the got in garden goose the

_____

_____

5. flew the goose winter for the south

_____

_____

6. is full there a moon tonight

_____

_____

Name _____

Double Vowel Words

Usually when two vowels appear together, the first one says its name and the second one is silent.
Example: b<u>ea</u>n

Directions: Unscramble the double vowel words below. Write the correct word on the line.

ocat ~~Ø~~coat

etar cry

mtea meat

eetf feet

teas seat

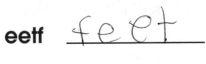
otab ~~so~~ boat

ogat goat

spea peas

atli tail

apil April

Your Total Solution for Second Grade

Vowel Teams

The vowel teams **ou** and **ow** can have the same sound. You can hear it in the words **clown** and **cloud**. The vowel teams **au** and **aw** have the same sound. You hear it in the words **because** and **law**.

Directions: Look at the pictures. Write the correct vowel team to complete the words. The first one is done for you. You may need to use a dictionary to help you with the correct spelling.

auto   cl_ow_n   h_ow_se

fl_ow_er   s_____   _ow_l

p_ow_der   m_ou_th   j_aw___

p_aw___   m_ou_se   cl_ou_d

Name _____

Vowel Teams

The vowel team **ea** can have a short **e** sound like in **head**, or a long **e** sound like in **bead**. An **ea** followed by an **r** makes a sound like the one in **ear** or like the one in **heard**.

Directions: Read the story. Listen for the sound **ea** makes in the bold words.

Have you ever **read** a book or **heard** a story about a **bear**? You might have **learned** that bears sleep through the winter. Some bears may sleep the whole **season**. Sometimes they look almost **dead**! But they are very much alive. As the cold winter passes and the spring **weather** comes **near**, they wake up. After such a nice rest, they must be **ready** to **eat** a **really** big **meal**!

words with long **ea**	words with short **ea**	**ea** followed by **r**
_____	_____	_____
_____	_____	_____
_____	_____	_____
_____	_____	_____

Your Total Solution for Second Grade

Vowel Teams

The vowel team **ie** makes the long **e** sound like in **believe**. The team **ei** also makes the long **e** sound like in **either**. But **ei** can also make a long **a** sound like in **eight**.

Directions: Circle the **ei** words with the long **a** sound.

(neighbor)   veil

(receive)   reindeer

reign   ceiling

The teams **eigh** and **ey** also make the long **a** sound.

Directions: Finish the sentences with words from the word box.

| chief | sleigh | obey | weigh | thief | field | ceiling |

1. Eight reindeer pull Santa's ___Sleigh___ .

2. Rules are for us to ___Obey___ .

3. The bird got out of its cage and flew up to the ___Ceiling___ .

4. The leader of an Indian tribe is the _____ .

5. How much do you ___Weigh___ ?

6. They caught the ___theif___ who took my bike.

7. Corn grows in a ___feild___ .

Name _____

Vowel Teams: oi, oy, ou, ow

Directions: Look at the first picture in each row. Circle the pictures that have the same sound.

© Carson-Dellosa • CD-704644

Your Total Solution for Second Grade

Vowel Teams: ai, ee

Directions: Write in the vowel team **ai** or **ee** to complete each word.

r _i_ _a_ n

f _o_ _o_ d

s _e_ _e_ d

p _h_ _i_ l

s _a_i_ l

cr _o_ _c_ k

Name _____

Compound Words

Compound words are formed by putting together two smaller words.

Directions: Help the cook brew her stew. Mix words from the first column with words from the second column to make new words. Write your new words on the lines at the bottom.

grand	brows
snow	light
eye	stairs
down	string
rose	book
shoe	mother
note	ball
moon	bud

1. _____

2. _____

3. _____

4. _____

5. _____

6. _____

7. _____

8. _____

Your Total Solution for Second Grade

Compound Words

Directions: Read the sentences. Fill in the blank with a compound word from the box.

raincoat   bedroom   lunchbox   hallway   sandbox

1. A box with sand is a

A sand Box with sand.

2. The way through a hall is a way to class

3. A box for lunch is a

snack for bag

4. A coat for the rain is a

raincoat

5. A room with a bed is a

bedroom

Name _____

Compound Words

Directions: Draw a line under the compound word in each sentence. On the line, write the two words that make up the compound word.

1. A firetruck came to help put out the fire.

_____

2. I will be nine years old on my next birthday.

_____

3. We built a treehouse at the back.

_____

4. Dad put a scarecrow in his garden.

_____

5. It is fun to make footprints in the snow.

_____

6. I like to read the comics in the newspaper.

_____

7. Cowboys ride horses and use lassos.

_____

Your Total Solution for Second Grade

Contractions

Contractions are a short way to write two words, such as **isn't**, **I've**, and **weren't**. Example: **it is = it's**

Directions: Draw a line from each word pair to its contraction.

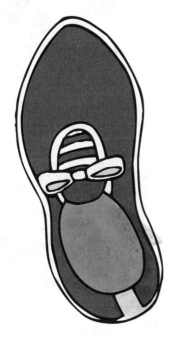 

I am	she's
it is	they're
you are	we're
we are	he's
they are	I'm
she is	it's
he is	you're

Name _____

Contractions

Directions: Circle the contraction that would replace the underlined words.

Example: were not = weren't

1. The boy _____was not_____ sad.
   wasn't   weren't

2. We _____were not_____ working.
   wasn't   weren't

3. Jen and Caleb _____have not_____ eaten lunch yet.
   haven't   hasn't

4. The mouse _____has not_____ been here.
   haven't   hasn't

Contractions

Directions: Match the words with their contractions.

would not   I've

was not   he'll

he will   wouldn't

could not   wasn't

I have   couldn't

Directions: Make the words at the end of each line into contractions to complete the sentences.

1. He _____ know the answer.   **did not**

2. _____ a long way home.   **It is**

3. _____ my house.   **Here is**

4. _____ not going to school today.   **We are**

5. _____ take the bus home tomorrow.   **They will**

Name _____

Syllables

Words are made up of parts called **syllables**. Each syllable has a vowel sound. One way to count syllables is to clap as you say the word.

Example:
cat	1 clap	1 syllable
table	2 claps	2 syllables
butterfly	3 claps	3 syllables

Directions: "Clap out" the words below. Write how many syllables each word has.

movie ___4___

piano ___3___

tree ___6___

bicycle ___7___

sun ___8___

cabinet ___9___

football ___10___

television ___11___

dog ___12___

basket ___13___

swimmer ___14___

rainbow ___15___

paper _____

picture _____

run _____

enter _____

Your Total Solution for Second Grade

Syllables

Dividing a word into syllables can help you read a new word. You also might divide syllables when you are writing if you run out of space on a line.

Many words contain two consonants that are next to each other. A word can usually be divided between the consonants.

Directions: Divide each word into two syllables. The first one is done for you.

kitten   <u> kit   ten </u>

lumber   _____

batter   _____

winter   _____

funny   _____

harder   _____

dirty   _____

sister   _____

little   _____

Name _____

Syllables

One way to help you read a word you don't know is to divide it into syllables. Every syllable has a vowel sound.

Directions: Say the words. Write the number of syllables. The first one is done for you.

straw • ber • ry

bird   _____1_____   rabbit   _____

apple   _____2_____   elephant   _____

balloon   _____2_____   family   _____

basketball   _____3_____   fence   _____

breakfast   _____2_____   ladder   _____

block   _____1_____   open   _____

candy   _____2_____   puddle   _____

popcorn   _____2_____   Saturday   _____

yellow   _____2_____   wind   _____

understand   _____3_____   butterfly   _____

Syllables

When a <u>double consonant</u> is used in the middle of a word, the word can usually be divided between the consonants.

Directions: Look at the words in the word box. Divide each word into two syllables. Leave space between each syllable. One is done for you.

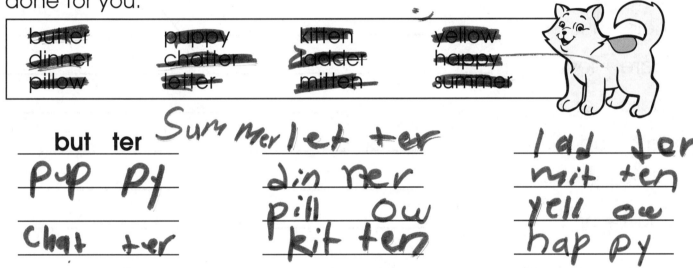

butter	puppy	kitten	yellow
dinner	chatter	ladder	happy
pillow	letter	mitten	summer

but   ter   Sum mer   let ter   lad ter

pup py   din ner   mit ten

        pill ow   yell ow

Chat ter   kit ten   hap py

Many words are divided between two consonants that are not alike.

Directions: Look at the words in the word box. Divide each word into two syllables. One is done for you.

window	doctor	number	carpet
mister	winter	pencil	candle
barber	sister	picture	under

win   dow

_____   _____   _____

_____   _____   _____

_____   _____   _____

Name _____

Suffixes

A **suffix** is a syllable that is added at the end of a word to change its meaning.

Directions: Add the suffixes to the root words to make new words. Use your new words to complete the sentences.

help + ful = _____

care + less = _____

build + er = _____

talk + ed = _____

love + ly = _____

loud + er = _____

1. My mother _____ to my teacher about my homework.

2. The radio was _____ than the television.

3. Sally is always _____ to her mother.

4. A _____ put a new garage on our house.

5. The flowers are _____.

6. It is _____ to cross the street without looking both ways.

Your Total Solution for Second Grade

Name _Siri_

Suffixes

Adding **ing** to a word means that it is happening now. Adding **ed** to a word means it happened in the past.

Directions: Look at the words in the word box. Underline the root word in each one. Write a word to complete each sentence.

snowing	wished	<u>played</u>	looking	crying
talking	walked	eating	going	doing

1. We like to play. We ___played___ yesterday.

2. Is that snow? Yes, it is ___Snowing___.

3. Do you want to go with me? No, I am ___walking___ with <u>my</u> friend.

4. The baby will cry if we leave. The baby is ___Crying___.

5. We will walk home from school. We ___go___ to school this morning.

6. Did you wish for a new bike? Yes, I _was_ ___Wising___ for one.

7. Who is going to do it while we are away? I am ___going to it___

8. Did you talk to your friend? Yes, we are ___talking___ now.

9. Will you look at my book? I am _____ at it now.

10. I like to eat pizza. We are _____ it today.

Name _____

Suffixes

Directions: Write a word from the word box next to its root word.

coming	running	sitting
lived	rained	swimming
visited	carried	racing
hurried		

run _____   come _____

live _____   carry _____

hurry _____   race _____

swim _____   rain _____

visit _____   sit _____

Directions: Write a word from the word box to finish each sentence.

1. I _____ my grandmother during vacation.

2. Mary went_____ at the lake with her cousin.

3. Jim_____ the heavy package for his mother.

4. It_____and stormed all weekend.

5. Cars go very fast when they are_____.

Your Total Solution for Second Grade

Name _____Siri_____

Prefixes: The Three R's

Prefixes are syllables added to the beginning of words that change their meaning. The prefix **re** means "again."

Directions: Read the story. Then, follow the instructions.

Kim wants to find ways she can save Earth. She studies the "three R's"—reduce, reuse, and recycle. **Reduce** means "to make less." Both **reuse** and **recycle** mean "to use again." Add **re** to the beginning of each word below. Use the new words to complete the sentences.

_____1_____ re build   _____3_____ re fill
_____5_____ re read   _____4_____ re tell
_____ re write   _____2_____ re run

1. The race was a tie, so Dawn and Kathy had to ___rerun___ it.

2. The block wall fell down, so Simon had to ___re build___ it.

3. The water bottle was empty, so Luna had to ___refill___ it.

4. Javier wrote a good story, but he wanted to ___retell___ it to make it better.

5. The teacher told a story, and students had to ___reread___ it.

6. Toni didn't understand the directions, so she had to

_____ them.

Name _____

Prefixes

Directions: Change the meaning of the sentences by adding the prefixes to the **bold** words.

The boy was **lucky** because he guessed the answer **correctly**.

The boy was (un) _____ because he guessed the

answer (in) _____ .

When Mary **behaved**, she felt **happy**.

When Mary (mis) _____ ,

she felt (un) _____ .

Mike wore his jacket **buttoned** because the dance was **formal**.

Mike wore his jacket (un) _____ because the dance

was (in) _____ .

Tim **understood** because he was **familiar** with the book.

Tim (mis) _____ because he was

(un) _____ with the book.

Your Total Solution for Second Grade

Synonyms

Words that mean the same or nearly the same are called **synonyms**.

Directions: Read the sentence that tells about the picture. Draw a circle around the word that means the same as the **bold** word.

The child is **unhappy**.

sad   hungry

The flowers are **lovely**.

pretty   green

The baby was very **tired**.

sleepy   hurt

The **funny** clown made us laugh

silly   glad

The ladybug is so **tiny**.

small   red

We saw a **scary** tiger.

frightening   ugly

Name _____

Synonyms

Directions: Read the story. Then, fill in the blanks with the synonyms.

| funny | unhappy |
| windy | little |

A New Balloon

It was a breezy day. The wind blew the small child's balloon away. The child was sad. A silly clown gave him a new balloon.

1. It was a _____ day.

2. The wind blew the _____ child's balloon away.

3. The child was _____.

4. A _____ clown gave him a new balloon.

Your Total Solution for Second Grade

Synonyms

Directions: Read each sentence. Fill in the blanks with the synonyms.

friend	tired	story
presents		little

I want to go to bed because I am very <u>sleepy</u>. _____

On my birthday, I like to open my <u>gifts</u>. _____

My <u>pal</u> and I like to play together. _____

My favorite <u>tale</u> is *Cinderella*. _____

The mouse was so <u>tiny</u> that it was hard to catch him. _____

Name _____

Antonyms

Antonyms are words that mean the opposite of another word.

Examples:
hot and **cold**
short and **tall**

Directions: Draw a line from each word on the left to its antonym on the right.

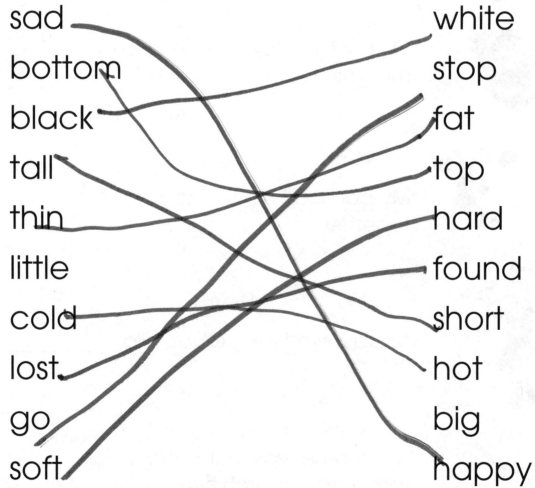

sad	white
bottom	stop
black	fat
tall	top
thin	hard
little	found
cold	short
lost	hot
go	big
soft	happy

Your Total Solution for Second Grade

Antonyms

Directions: Read the words next to the pictures. Draw a line to the antonyms.

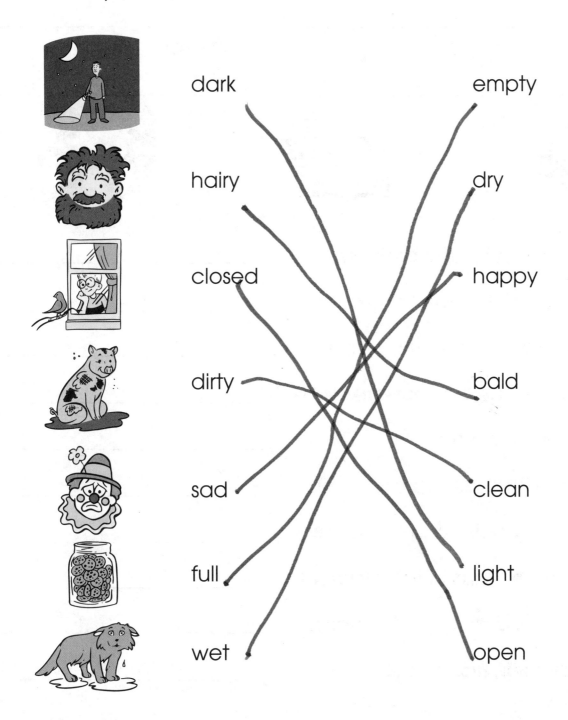

dark   empty

hairy   dry

closed   happy

dirty   bald

sad   clean

full   light

wet   open

Name _____

Antonyms

Directions: Read the sentence. Write the word from the word box that means the opposite of the **bold** word.

bottom	outside	black	summer	after
light	sister	clean	last	evening

1. Lisa has a new baby **brother**. _____

2. The class went **inside** for recess. _____

3. There is a **white** car in the driveway. _____

4. We went to the park **before** dinner. _____

5. Joe's puppy is **dirty**. _____

6. My name is at the **top** of the list. _____

7. I like to play outside in the **winter**. _____

8. I like to take walks in the **morning**. _____

9. The sky was **dark** after the storm. _____

10. Our team is in **first** place. _____

Your Total Solution for Second Grade

Homophones

Homophones are words that sound the same but are spelled differently and mean different things.

Directions: Write the homophone from the box next to each picture.

so	see	blew	pear

sew _____

pair _____

sea _____

blue _____

Name _____

Homophones

Directions: Look at each picture. Circle the correct homophone.

(deer)   dear

(two)   to

by   (bye)

ate   (eight)

blue (blew)

hi (high)

(new) knew

(red) read

Your Total Solution for Second Grade

Name _____

Homophones

Directions: Match each word with its homophone.

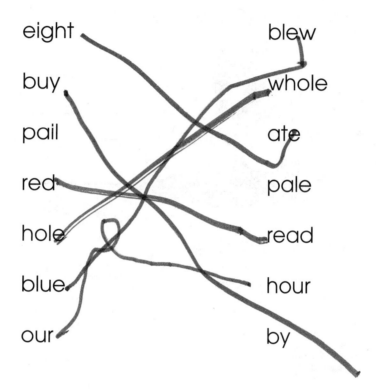

eight   blew

buy   whole

pail   ate

red   pale

hole   read

blue   hour

our   by

Directions: Choose three homophone pairs and write sentences using them.

1. _____

2. _____

3. _____

© Carson-Dellosa • CD-704644

Name _____ R i th wi R

Nouns

A **noun** is the name of a person, place, or thing.

Directions: Read the story and circle all the nouns. Then, write the nouns next to the pictures below.

Our family likes to go to the park.

We play on the swings.

plural Nouns

We eat cake.

We drink lemonade.

We throw the ball to our dog.

Then, we go home.

_____

_____

_____

_____

_____

_____

© Carson-Dellosa • CD-704644

Your Total Solution for Second Grade

Proper Nouns

Proper nouns are the names of specific people, places, and pets. Proper nouns begin with a capital letter.

Directions: Write the proper nouns on the lines below. Use capital letters at the beginning of each word.

logan, utah

mike smith

lynn cramer

buster

fluffy

chicago, illinois

Name _____

Proper Nouns

The days of the week and the months of the year are proper nouns.

Directions: Circle the words that are written correctly. Write the words that need capital letters on the lines below.

sunday	July	Wednesday	may	Monday
friday	tuesday	june	august	April
january	February	March	Thursday	
September	saturday	October	december	

Days of the Week

1. Monday

2. tuse day

3. wednesday

4. thursday

Months of the Year

1. Jan

2. feb

3. march

4. april

5. may

Your Total Solution for Second Grade

Proper Nouns

The first word and all of the important words in a title begin with a capital letter.

Directions: Write the book titles on the lines below. Use capital letters.

1. Dinosaurs

2. lizards everywhere

3. the magic cat

4. all about presidents

5. the space dog

6. gerbil - care

Name _____

Plural Nouns

Plural nouns name more than one person, place, or thing.

Directions: Read the words in the box. Write the words in the correct column.

~~hats~~	gift	~~cows~~	kittens	cake
~~spoons~~	glass	book	horse	trees

one

more than one

girl   hats

_____   _____

glass   spoons

_____   _____

DOOR   Cows

_____   _____

_____   _____

_____   _____

     Your Total Solution for Second Grade

Plurals

Plurals are words that mean more than one. You usually add an **s** or **es** to the word. In some words ending in **y**, the **y** changes to an **i** before adding **es**. For example, **baby** changes to **babies**.

Directions: Look at the following lists of plural words. Write the word that means one next to it. The first one has been done for you.

foxes	**fox**
bushes	bush
dresses	dress
chairs	chair
shoes	shoe
stories	story
puppies	puppy
matches	match
cars	car
glasses	glass

balls	ball
candles	candle
wishes	wish
boxes	box
ladies	lady
bunnies	bunny
desks	desk
dishes	dish
pencils	pencil
trucks	truck

Name _____

More Than One

To show more than one of something, we add **s** to most words.
Example: one dog – **two dogs**   one book – **two books**
But some words are different. For words that end with **x**, use **es** to show two.
Example: one fox – **two foxes**   one box – **two boxes**
The spelling of some words changes a lot when there are two.
Example: one mouse – **two mice**
Some words stay the same, even when you mean two of something.
Example: one deer – **two deer**   one fish – **two fish**

Directions: Complete the sentences below with the correct word.

1. The [rabbits] run fast.   _____

2. The [deer] are eating   _____

3. Have you seen any [bears] today?   _____

4. Where do the [foxes] live?   _____

5. Did you ever have [mice] for pets?   _____

Your Total Solution for Second Grade

Pronouns

Pronouns are words that can be used instead of nouns. **She**, **he**, **it**, and **they** are pronouns.

Directions: Read the sentence. Then, write the sentence again, using **she**, **he**, **it**, or **they** in the blank.

1. Dan likes funny jokes. _____ likes funny jokes.

2. Peg and Sam went to the zoo. _____ went to the zoo.

3. My dog likes to dig in the yard. _____ likes to dig in the yard.

4. Sara is a very good dancer. _____ is a very good dancer.

5. Fred and Ted are twins. _____ are twins.

Name _____

Verbs

A **verb** is the action word in a sentence. Verbs tell what something does or that something exists.

Example: Run, sleep, and **jump** are verbs.

Directions: Circle the verbs in the sentences below.

1. We play baseball everyday.

2. Susan pitches the ball very well.

3. Mike swings the bat harder than anyone.

4. Chris slides into home base.

5. Laura hit a home run.

Your Total Solution for Second Grade

Verbs

We use verbs to tell when something happens. Sometimes we add an **ed** to verbs that tell us if something has already happened.

Example: Today, we will **play**. Yesterday, we **played**.

Directions: Write the correct verb in the blank.

1. Today, I will _____ my dog, Fritz.

      wash washed

2. Last week, Fritz _____ when we said, "Bath time, Fritz."

      cry cried

3. My sister likes to _____ wash Fritz.

      help helped

4. One time she _____ Fritz by herself.

      clean cleaned

5. Fritz will _____ a lot better after his bath.

    look looked

Verbs: Sentences

Directions: Read the two sentences in each story below. Then, write one more sentence to tell what happened next. Use the verbs from the box.

break	build	fix	clean	cut	carry

Today is Mike's birthday.

Mike asked four friends to come.

_____

Edith's dog walked in the mud.

He got mud in the house.

_____

Is, Are, and Am

Is, **are**, and **am** are special action words that tell us something is happening now.

Use **am** with **I**. **Example: I am**.
Use **is** to tell about one person or thing. **Example: He is**.
Use **are** to tell about more than one. **Example: We are**.
Use **are** with you. **Example: You are**.

Directions: Write **is**, **are**, or **am** in the sentences below.

1. My friends _____ helping me build a tree house.

2. It _____ in my backyard.

3. We _____ using hammers, wood, and nails.

4. It _____ a very hard job.

5. I _____ lucky to have good friends.

Name _____

Was and Were

Was and **were** tell us about something that already happened.

Use **was** to tell about one person or thing. **Example: I was, he was.**
Use **were** to tell about more than one person or thing or when using
the word **you. Example: We were, you were.**

Directions: Write **was** or **were** in each sentence.

1. Lily _____ eight years old on her birthday.

2. Tim and Steve _____ happy to be at the party.

3. Megan _____ too shy to sing "Happy Birthday."

4. Ben _____ sorry he dropped his cake.

5. All of the children _____ happy to be invited.

Your Total Solution for Second Grade

Go, Going, and Went

We use **go** or **going** to tell about now or later. Sometimes we use **going** with the words **am** or **are**. We use **went** to tell about something that already happened.

Directions: Write **go**, **going**, or **went** in the sentences below.

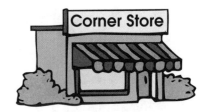

1. Today, I will _____ to the store.

2. Yesterday, we _____ shopping.

3. I am _____ to take Muffy to the vet.

4. Jan and Steve _____ to the party.

5. They are _____ to have a good day.

Name _____

Have, Has, and Had

We use **have** and **has** to tell about now. We use **had** to tell about something that already happened.

Directions: Write **has**, **have**, or **had** in the sentences below.

1. We _____ three cats at home.

2. Ginger _____ brown fur.

3. Bucky and Charlie _____ gray fur.

4. My friend Tom _____ one cat, but he died.

5. Tom _____ a new cat now.

Your Total Solution for Second Grade

See, Saw, and Sees

We use **see** or **sees** to tell about now. We use **saw** to tell about something that already happened.

Directions: Write **see**, **sees**, or **saw** in the sentences below.

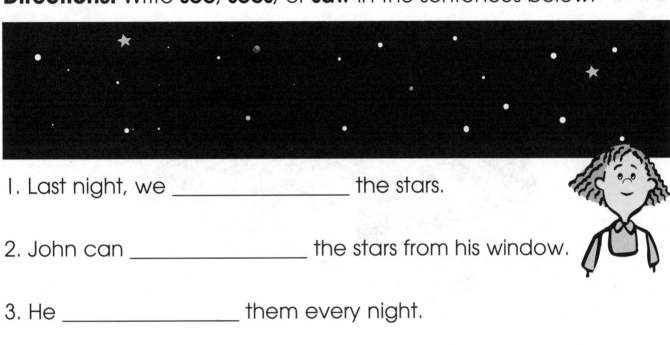

1. Last night, we _____ the stars.

2. John can _____ the stars from his window.

3. He _____ them every night.

4. Last week, he _____ the Big Dipper.

5. Can you _____ it in the night sky, too?

6. If you _____ it, you would remember it!

7. John _____ it often now.

8. How often do you _____ it?

Name _____

Eat, Eats, and Ate

We use **eat** or **eats** to tell about now. We use **ate** to tell about what already happened.

Directions: Write **eat**, **eats**, or **ate** in the sentences below.

1. We like to _____ in the lunchroom.

2. Today, my teacher will _____ in a different room.

3. She _____ with the other teachers.

4. Yesterday, we _____ pizza, pears, and peas.

5. Today, we will _____ turkey and potatoes.

Your Total Solution for Second Grade

Leave, Leaves, and Left

We use **leave** and **leaves** to tell about now. We use **left** to tell about what already happened.

Directions: Write **leave**, **leaves**, or **left** in the sentences below.

1. Last winter, we _____ seeds in the bird feeder everyday.

2. My mother likes to _____ food out for the squirrels.

3. When it rains, she _____ bread for the birds.

4. Yesterday, she _____ popcorn for the birds.

© Carson-Dellosa • CD-704644

Name _____

Adjectives

Adjectives are words that tell more about a person, place, or thing.

Examples: cold, fuzzy, dark

Directions: Circle the adjectives in the sentences.

1. The juicy apple is on the plate.

2. The furry dog is eating a bone.

3. It was a sunny day.

4. The kitten drinks warm milk.

5. The baby has a loud cry.

Your Total Solution for Second Grade

Adjectives

Directions: Choose an adjective from the box to fill in the blanks.

hungry	sunny	busy	funny
fresh	deep	pretty	cloudy

1. It is a _____ day on Farmer Brown's farm.

2. Farmer Brown is a very _____ man.

3. Mrs. Brown likes to feed the _____ chickens.

4. Every day she collects the _____ eggs.

5. The ducks swim in the _____ pond.

Name _Siri_

Adjectives

Directions: Think of your own adjectives. Write a story about Fluffy the cat.

1. Fluffy is a _____cute_____ cat.

2. The color of his fur is _____orange_____.

3. He likes to chew on my _____faveroit_____ *favourite* shoes.

4. He likes to eat _____his_____ cat food.

5. I like Fluffy because he is so _____adorable_____.

Your Total Solution for Second Grade

Subjects

The **subject** of a sentence is the person, place, or thing the sentence is about.

Directions: Underline the subject in each sentence.

Example: Mom read a book.
(Think: Who is the sentence about? <u>Mom</u>)

1. The bird flew away.

2. The kite was high in the air.

3. The children played a game.

4. The books fell down.

5. The monkey climbed a tree.

Name _____

Compound Subjects

Two similar sentences can be joined into one sentence if the predicate is the same. A **compound subject** is made up of two subjects joined together by the word **and**.

Example: Jamie can sing.
Sandy can sing.
<u>Jamie **and** Sandy</u> can sing.

Directions: Combine the sentences. Write the new sentence on the line.

1. The cats are my pets.
The dogs are my pets.

_____

2. Chairs are in the store.
Tables are in the store.

_____

3. Tom can ride a bike
Jack can ride a bike.

_____

Your Total Solution for Second Grade

Predicates

The **predicate** is the part of the sentence that tells about the action.

Directions: Circle the predicate in each sentence.

Example: The boys ran on the playground.
(Think: The boys did what? (Ran))

1. The woman (painted) a picture.

2. The puppy (chases) his ball.

3. The (students) went to school.

4. (Butterflies) fly in the air.

5. The (baby) wants a (drink).

Name _____

Subjects and Predicates

The **subject** part of the sentence is the person, place, or thing the sentence is about. The **predicate** is the part of the sentence that tells what the subject does.

Directions: Draw a line between the subject and the predicate. Underline the noun in the subject and circle the verb.

Example: The furry <u>cat</u> | (ate) food.

1. Mandi walks to school.

2. The bus drove the children.

3. The school bell rang very (loudly).

4. The teacher spoke to the (students).

5. The girls opened their books.

            Your Total Solution for Second Grade

Parts of a Sentence

Directions: Draw a circle around the noun, the naming part of the sentence. Draw a line under the verb, the action part of the sentence.

Example: (John) <u>drinks</u> juice every morning.

1. Our class skates at the roller-skating rink.

2. Mike and Jan go very fast.

3. Fred eats hot dogs.

4. Sue dances to the music.

5. Everyone likes the skating rink.

© Carson-Dellosa • CD-704644

Name _____

Parts of a Sentence

Directions: Look at the pictures. Draw a line from the naming part of the sentence to the action part to complete the sentence.

The boy   delivered the mail.

A small dog   threw a football.

The mailman   fell down.

The goalie   chased the ball.

Your Total Solution for Second Grade

Sentences and Non-Sentences

A **sentence** tells a complete idea. It has a noun and a verb. It begins with a capital letter and has punctuation at the end.

Directions: Circle the group of words if it is a sentence.

1. Grass is a green plant.

2. Mowing the lawn.

3. Grass grows in fields and lawns.

4. Tickle the feet.

5. Sheep, cows, and horses eat grass.

6. We like to play in.

7. My sister likes to mow the lawn.

8. A picnic on the grass.

9. My dog likes to roll in the grass.

10. Plant flowers around.

Name _____

Sentences and Non-Sentences

Directions: Circle the group of words if it tells a complete idea.

1. A secret is something you know.

2. My mom's birthday gift is a secret.

3. No one else.

4. If you promise not to.

5. I'll tell you a secret.

6. Something nobody knows.

Your Total Solution for Second Grade

Statements

Statements are sentences that tell us something. They begin with a capital letter and end with a period.

Directions: Write the sentences on the lines below. Begin each sentence with a capital letter and end it with a period.

1. we like to ride our bikes

We like to ride our bikes.

2. we go down the hill very fast

_____

3. we keep our bikes shiny and clean

_____

4. we know how to change the tires

_____

Name _____

Surprising Sentences

Surprising sentences tell a strong feeling and end with an exclamation point. A surprising sentence may be only one or two words showing fear, surprise, or pain. **Example: Oh, no!**

Directions: Put a period at the end of the sentences that tell something. Put an exclamation point at the end of the sentences that tell a strong feeling. Put a question mark at the end of the sentences that ask a question.

1. The cheetah can run very fast

2. Wow

3. Look at that cheetah go

4. Can you run fast

5. Oh, my

6. You're faster than I am

7. Let's run together

8. We can run as fast as a cheetah

9. What fun

10. Do you think cheetahs get tired

Your Total Solution for Second Grade

Name _____

Commands

Commands tell someone to do something. **Example: "Be careful."**
It can also be written as "Be careful!" if it tells a strong feeling.

Directions: Put a period at the end of the command sentences.
Use an exclamation point if the sentence tells a strong feeling.
Write your own commands on the lines below.

1. Clean your room

2. Now

3. Be careful with your goldfish

4. Watch out

5. Be a little more careful

_____

_____

Name _____

Questions

Questions are sentences that ask something. They begin with a capital letter and end with a question mark.

Directions: Write the questions on the lines below. Begin each sentence with a capital letter and end it with a question mark.

1. will you be my friend

_____

2. what is your name

_____

3. are you eight years old

_____

4. do you like rainbows

_____

Your Total Solution for Second Grade

Ownership

We add **'s** to nouns (people, places, or things) to tell who or what owns something.

Directions: Read the sentences. Fill in the blanks to show ownership.

Example: The doll belongs to **Sara**.
It is **Sara's** doll.

1. Sparky has a red collar.

_____ collar is red.

2. Jimmy has a blue coat.

_____ coat is blue.

3. The tail of the cat is short.

The _____ tail is short.

4. The name of my mother is Karen.

My _____ name is Karen.

Name _____

Ownership

Directions: Read the sentences. Choose the correct word and write it in the sentences below.

1. The _boy's_ lunchbox is broken. boys (boy's)

2. The _birds_ played in the cage. gerbil's gerbils

3. _ann's_ hair is brown. ~~Anns~~ ~~Ann's~~

4. The _____ ran in the field. horse's horses

5. My _____ coat is torn. sister's sisters

6. The _____ fur is brown. cats cat's

7. Three _____ flew past our window. (birds) (bird's)

8. The _____ paws are muddy. dogs dog's

9. The _____ neck is long. giraffes giraffe's

10. The _____ are big and powerful. lion's lions

Your Total Solution for Second Grade

Following Directions

Directions: Read the story. Answer the questions. Try the recipe.

Cows Give Us Milk

Cows live on a farm. The farmer milks the cow to get milk. Many things are made from milk. We make ice cream, sour cream, cottage cheese, and butter from milk. Butter is fun to make! You can learn to make your own butter. First, you need cream. Put the cream in a jar and shake it. Then, you need to pour off the liquid. Next, you put the butter in a bowl. Add a little salt and stir! Finally, spread it on crackers and eat!

1. What animal gives us milk? _____

2. What four things are made from milk?

_____ _____ _____ _____

3. What did the story teach you to make? _____

4. Put the steps in order. Write **1**, **2**, **3**, and **4** by the sentences.

_____ Spread the butter on crackers and eat!

_____ Shake cream in a jar.

_____ Start with cream.

_____ Add salt to the butter.

Name _____

Following Directions: Ladybugs

Directions: Read about how to treat ladybugs. Then, follow the instructions.

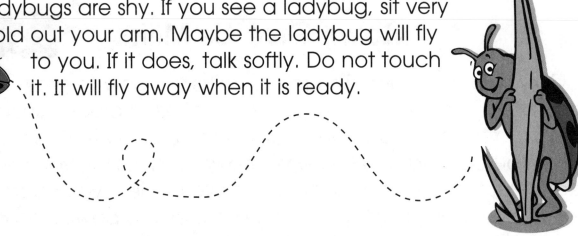

Ladybugs are shy. If you see a ladybug, sit very still. Hold out your arm. Maybe the ladybug will fly to you. If it does, talk softly. Do not touch it. It will fly away when it is ready.

1. Complete the directions on how to treat a ladybug.

   a. Sit very still.

   b. _____

   c. Talk softly.

   d. _____

2. Ladybugs are red. They have black spots. Color the ladybug.

Your Total Solution for Second Grade

Sequencing: Packing Bags

Directions: Read about packing bags. Then, number the objects in the order they should be packed.

Cans are heavy. Put them in first. Then, put in boxes. Now, put in the apple. Put the bread in last.

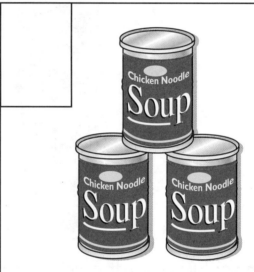

Name _Siri_

Sequencing: Story Events

Spencer likes to make new friends. Today, he made friends with the dog in the picture.

Directions: Number the sentences in order to find out what Spencer did today.

____ Spencer kissed his mother good-bye.

____ Spencer saw the new dog next door.

____ Spencer went outside.

____ Spencer said hello.

____ Spencer got dressed and ate breakfast.

____ Spencer woke up.

Your Total Solution for Second Grade

Sequencing: Yo-Yo Trick

Directions: Read about the yo-yo trick.

Wind up the yo-yo string. Hold the yo-yo in your hand. Now, hold your palm up. Throw the yo-yo downward on the string. Hold your palm down. Now, swing the yo-yo forward. Make it "walk." This yo-yo trick is called "Walk the Dog."

Directions: Number the directions in order.

_____3_____ Swing the yo-yo forward and make it "walk."

_____1_____ Hold your palm up and drop the yo-yo.

_____2_____ Turn your palm down as the yo-yo reaches the ground.

Name _____

Sequencing: Story Events

Mari was sick yesterday.

Directions: Number the events in 1, 2, 3 order to tell the story about Mari.

3 ___ She went to the doctor's office.

___ Mari felt much better.

1 ___ Mari felt very hot and tired.

2 ___ Mari's mother went to the drugstore.

5 ___ The doctor wrote down something.

4 ___ The doctor looked in Mari's ears.

6 ___ Mari took a pill.

7 ___ The doctor gave Mari's mother the piece of paper.

8 ___ Mari drank some water with her pill.

Your Total Solution for Second Grade

Sequencing: Making Clay

Directions: Read about making clay. Then, follow the instructions.

It is fun to work with clay. Here is what you need to make it:

1 cup salt
2 cups flour
$\frac{3}{4}$ cup water

Mix the salt and flour. Then, add the water. DO NOT eat the clay. It tastes bad. Use your hands to mix and mix. Now, roll it out. What can you make with your clay?

1. Circle the main idea:

Do not eat clay.

Mix salt, flour, and water to make clay.

2. Write the steps for making clay.

a. _____

b. _____

c. Mix the clay.

d. _____

3. Write why you should not eat clay. _____

_____

Name _____

Sequencing: A Visit to the Zoo

Directions: Read the story. Then, follow the instructions.

One Saturday morning in May, Gloria and Anna went to the zoo. First, they bought tickets to get into the zoo. Second, they visited the Gorilla Garden and had fun watching the gorillas stare at them. Then, they went to Tiger Town and watched the tigers as they slept in the sunshine. Fourth, they went to Hippo Haven and laughed at the hippos cooling off in their pool. Next, they visited Snake Station and learned about poisonous and nonpoisonous snakes. It was noon, and they were hungry, so they ate lunch at the Parrot Patio.

Write **first**, **second**, **third**, **fourth**, **fifth**, and **sixth** to put the events in order.

__4__ They went to Hippo Haven.

__1__ Gloria and Anna bought zoo tickets.

__3__ They watched the tigers sleep.

__6__ They ate lunch at Parrot Patio.

__2__ The gorillas stared at them.

__5__ They learned about poisonous and nonpoisonous snakes.

Your Total Solution for Second Grade

Same and Different: Stuffed Animals

Kate and Oralia like to collect and trade stuffed animals.

Directions: Draw two stuffed animals that are alike and two that are different.

Alike

Different

Name _____

Same and Different: Cats and Tigers

Directions: Read about cats and tigers. Then, complete the Venn diagram, telling how they are the same and different.

Tigers are a kind of cat. Pet cats and tigers both have fur. Pet cats are small and tame. Tigers are large and wild.

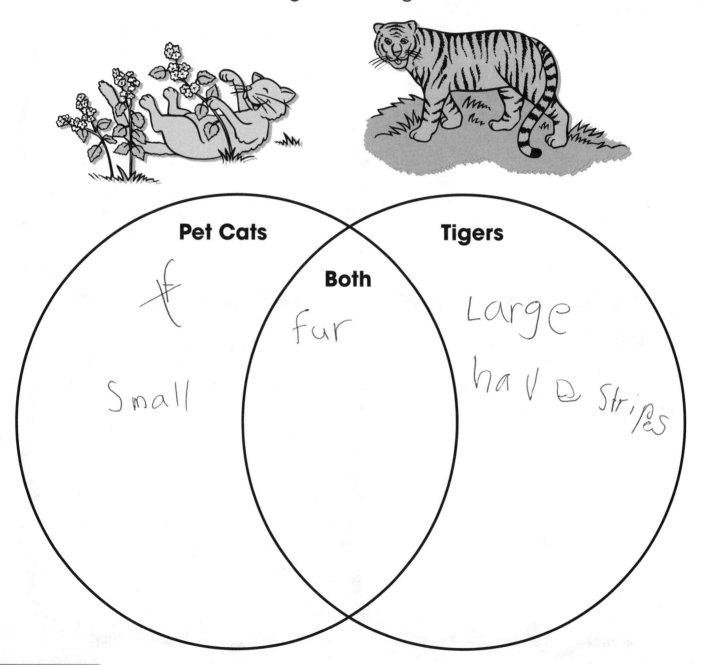

Pet Cats

Tigers

Both

Small

fur

Large

have stripes

Your Total Solution for Second Grade

Same and Different: Birds

Directions: Read about parrots and bluebirds. Then, complete the Venn diagram, telling how they are the same and different.

Bluebirds and parrots are both birds. Bluebirds and parrots can fly. They both have beaks. Parrots can live inside a cage. Bluebirds must live outdoors.

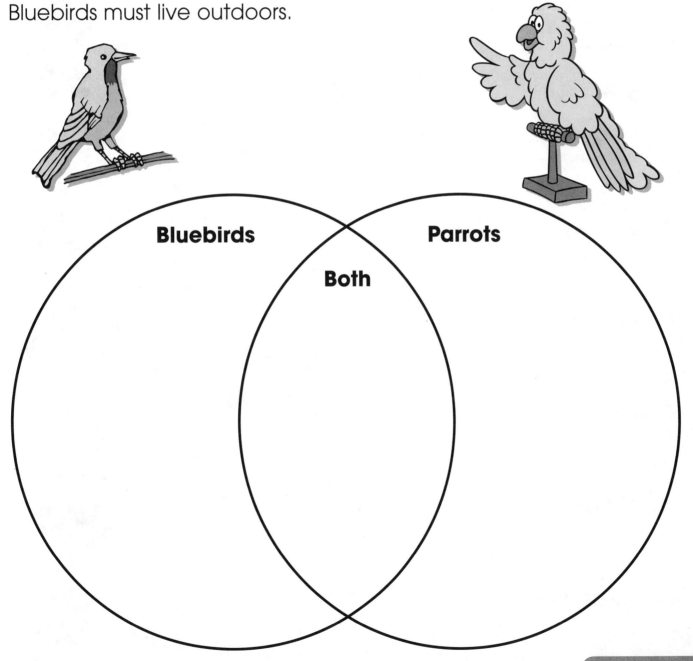

Bluebirds

Both

Parrots

© Carson-Dellosa • CD-704644

Name _____

Similes

A **simile** is a figure of speech that compares two different things. The words **like** or **as** are used in similes.

Directions: Draw a line to the picture that goes with each set of words.

as hard as a

as hungry as a

as quiet as a

as soft as a

as easy as

as light as a

as tiny as an

Your Total Solution for Second Grade

Name _____

Classifying: Outdoor/Indoor Games

Classifying is putting things that are alike into groups.

Directions: Read about games. Draw an **X** on the games you can play indoors. Circle the objects used for outdoor games.

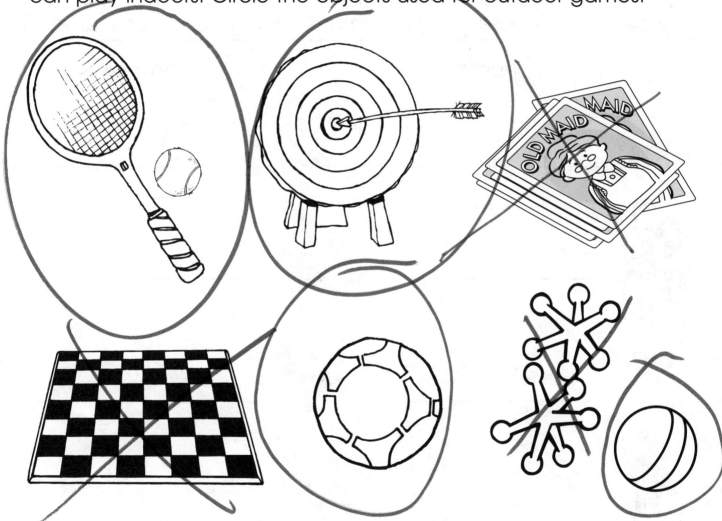

Some games are outdoor games. Some games are indoor games. Outdoor games are active. Indoor games are quiet.

Which do you like best? _____ indoors _____

Name _____

Classifying

Directions: Write each word from the word box on the correct line.

~~baby~~	donkey	whale	family	fox
uncle	goose	grandfather	kangaroo	policeman

people

animals

baby

goose

family

whale

gandfather
uncle and

fox

police man

Kangaroo

uncle

Donky

Your Total Solution for Second Grade

Classifying: Animals

Directions: Use a red crayon to circle the names of three animals that would make good pets. Use a blue crayon to circle the names of three wild animals. Use an orange crayon to circle the two animals that live on a farm.

BEAR CAT LION SHEEP BIRD DOG COW TIGER

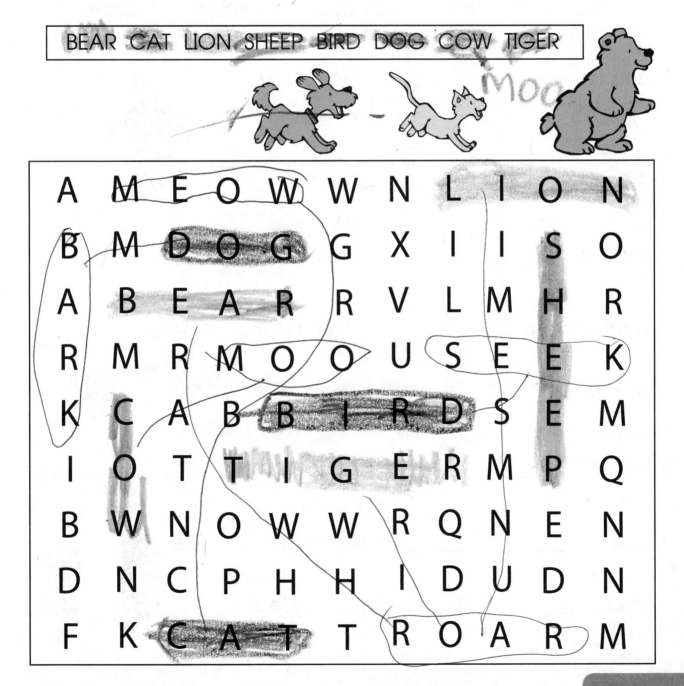

A M E O W W N L I O N
B M D O G G X I I S O
A B E A R R V L M H R
R M R M O O U S E E K
K C A B B I R D S E M
I O T T I G E R M P Q
B W N O W W R Q N E N
D N C P H H I D U D N
F K C A T T R O A R M

Name _____

Opposite Words

Directions: Opposites are words that are different in every way. Use the opposite word from the box to complete these sentences.

hard	hot	bottom	quickly	happy
sad	slowly	cold	soft	top

Example:

My new coat is blue on __top__ and

red on the __bottom__ .

1. Snow is _____ , but fire is _____ .

2. A rabbit runs _____ , but a turtle

   moves _____ .

3. A bed is _____ , but a floor is _____ .

4. I feel _____ when my friends come

   and _____ when they leave.

Your Total Solution for Second Grade

Opposite Words

Directions: Draw a line from each sentence to its picture. Then, complete each sentence with the word under the picture.

Example:

She bought a __new__ bat.

hard

1. I like my _____ pillow.

new

2. Birthdays make me _____.

top

3. Put that book on _____.

sad

4. Jenny runs _____.

slowly

5. A rock makes a _____ seat.

quickly

6. I feel _____ when it rains.

happy

7. He eats _____.

soft

© Carson-Dellosa • CD-704644

Name _____

Comprehension: Types of Tops

The **main idea** is the most important point or idea in a story.

Directions: Read about tops. Then, answer the questions.

Tops come in all sizes. Some tops are made of wood. Some tops are made of tin. All tops do the same thing. They spin! Do you have a top?

1. Circle the main idea:

   There are many kinds of tops.

   Some tops are made of wood.

2. What are some tops made of? _____

3. What do all tops do? _____

   Your Total Solution for Second Grade

Comprehension: The Puppet Play

Directions: Read the play out loud with a friend. Then, answer the questions.

Pip: Hey, Pep. What kind of turkey eats very fast?

Pep: Uh, I don't know.

Pip: A gobbler!

Pep: I have a good joke for you, Pip. What kind of burger does a polar bear eat?

Pip: Uh, a cold burger?

Pep: No, an iceberg-er!

Pip: Hey, that was a great joke!

1. Who are the characters in the play?_____

    _____

2. Who are the jokes about?_____

    _____

3. What are the characters in the play doing?_____

    _____

Name _____

Comprehension: Snakes!

Directions: Read about snakes. Then, answer the questions.

There are many facts about snakes that might surprise someone. A snake's skin is dry. Most snakes are shy. They will hide from people. Snakes eat mice and rats. They do not chew them up. Snakes' jaws drop open to swallow their food whole.

1. How does a snake's skin feel? __dry__

2. Most snakes are __Shy,__ .

3. What do snakes eat?

a. __mice__

b. __rats__

Your Total Solution for Second Grade

Comprehension: Sean's Basketball Game

Directions: Read about Sean's basketball game. Then, answer the questions.

Sean really likes to play basketball. One sunny day, he decided to ask his friends to play basketball at the park, but there were six people—Sean, Aki, Lance, Kate, Zac, and Oralia. A basketball team only allows five to play at a time. So, Sean decided to be the coach. Sean and his friends had fun.

1. How many kids wanted to play basketball? _____

2. Write their names in ABC order:

    _____ _____ _____

    _____ _____ _____

3. How many players can play on a basketball

    team at a time? _____

4. Where did they play basketball? _____

5. Who decided to be the coach? _____

Name _____

Comprehension: Amazing Ants

Directions: Read about ants. Then, answer the questions.

Ants are insects. Ants live in many parts of the world and make their homes in soil, sand, wood, and leaves. Most ants live for about 6 to 10 weeks. But the queen ant, who lays the eggs, can live for up to 15 years!

The largest ant is the bulldog ant. This ant can grow to be 5 inches long, and it eats meat! The bulldog ant can be found in Australia.

1. Where do ants make their homes? _Soil Sand_
   wood and Leave

2. How long can a queen ant live? _15 years_
   _____

3. What is the largest ant? _Bull Dog ant_

4. What does it eat? _meat_

Your Total Solution for Second Grade

Comprehension: Fish

Directions: Read about fish. Then, follow the instructions.

Some fish live in warm water. Some live in cold water. Some fish live in lakes. Some fish live in oceans. There are 20,000 kinds of fish!

1. Name two types of water in which fish live.

   a. _Warm water._

   b. _cold water._

   Some fish live in lakes and some live in __Oceans__.

2. Name another place fish live __Lakes__

3. There are __20,000__ kinds of fish.

Name _____

Predicting: A Rainy Game

Predicting is telling what is likely to happen based on the facts.

Directions: Read the story. Then, check each sentence below that tells how the story could end.

One cloudy day, Juan and his baseball team, the Bears, played the Crocodiles. It was the last half of the fifth inning, and it started to rain. The coaches and umpires had to decide what to do.

_____ They kept playing until nine innings were finished.

_____ They ran for cover and waited until the rain stopped.

_____ Each player grabbed an umbrella and returned to the field to finish the game.

_____ They canceled the game and played it another day.

_____ They acted like crocodiles and slid around the wet bases.

_____ The coaches played the game while the players sat in the dugout.

Your Total Solution for Second Grade

Predicting: Dog Derby

Directions: Read the story. Then, answer the questions.

Marcy had a great idea for a game to play with her dogs, Marvin and Mugsy. The game was called "Dog Derby." Marcy would stand at one end of the driveway and hold on to the dogs by their collars. Her friend Mitch would stand at the other end of the driveway. When he said, "Go!" Marcy would let go of the dogs and they would race to Mitch. The first one there would get a dog biscuit. If there was a tie, both dogs would get a biscuit.

1. Who do you think will win the race?

_____ marvin!_____

Why? _____ a fast Dog_____

_____

2. What do you think will happen when they race again?

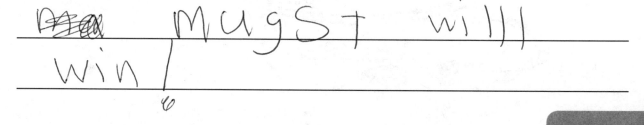

_____ Mugst will_____

_____ win_____

Name _____ Bodapati

Predicting: Dog-Gone!

Directions: Read the story. Then, follow the instructions.

Scotty and Simone were washing their dog, Willis. His fur was wet. Their hands were wet. Willis did not like to be wet. Scotty dropped the soap. Simone picked it up and let go of Willis. Uh-oh!

1. Write what happened next.

_____

_____

_____

2. Draw what happened next.

    Your Total Solution for Second Grade

Predicting: At the Zoo

Directions: Read the story. Complete the story in the last box.

1. "Look at that elephant!
   He sure is big!"

2. "I'm hungry."
   "I bet that elephant is, too."

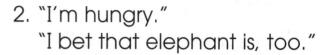

3. "Stop, Amy! Look at that sign!"

4. _Only the zoo keepers are allowed to feed them_

Name _____

Predicting: Windy Days

Directions: Complete the story. Then, draw pictures to match the four parts.

1. Sylvia and Marge are flying a kite.

2. The kite gets stuck in a tree.

Beginning

Middle

3._____

_____

4._____

_____

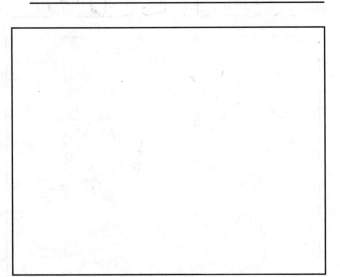

Middle

End

Your Total Solution for Second Grade

Predicting: Fun at the Fair

Kelly and Gina always have fun at the fair.

Directions: Read the sentences.
Write what you think will happen next.

1. Kelly and Gina are riding the Ferris wheel. It stops when they are at the top.

_____

_____

_____

2. As they walk into the animal barn, a little piglet runs toward them.

_____

_____

_____

3. Snow cones are their favorite way to cool off. The ones they bought are made from real snow.

_____

_____

_____

4. They play a "toss the ring over the bottle" game, but when the ring goes around the bottle, it disappears.

_____

_____

_____

Name _____

Fact and Opinion: Recycling

Directions: Read about recycling. Then, follow the instructions.

What do you throw away every day? What could you do with these things? You could change an old greeting card into a new card. You could make a puppet with an old paper bag. Old buttons make great refrigerator magnets. You can plant seeds in plastic cups. Cardboard tubes make perfect rockets. So, use your imagination!

1. Write **F** next to each fact and **O** next to each opinion.

_____ Cardboard tubes are ugly.

_____ Buttons can be made into refrigerator magnets.

_____ An old greeting card can be changed into a new card.

_____ Paper-bag puppets are cute.

_____ Seeds can be planted in plastic cups.

_____ Rockets can be made from cardboard tubes.

2. What could you do with a cardboard tube? _____

Your Total Solution for Second Grade

Name _____

Fact and Opinion: An Owl Story

Directions: Read the story. Then, follow the instructions.

My name is Owen Owl, and I am a bird. I go to Nocturnal School. Our teacher is Mr. Screech Owl. In his class I learned that owls are birds and can sleep all day and hunt at night. Some of us live in nests in trees. In North America, it is against the law to harm owls. I like being an owl!

Write **F** next to each fact and **O** next to each opinion.

_____ 1. No one can harm owls in North America.

_____ 2. It would be great if owls could talk.

_____ 3. Owls sleep all day.

_____ 4. Some owls sleep in nests.

_____ 5. Mr. Screech Owl is a good teacher.

_____ 6. Owls are birds.

_____ 7. Owen Owl would be a good friend.

_____ 8. Owls hunt at night.

_____ 9. Nocturnal School is a good school for smart owls.

_____ 10. This story is for the birds.

Name _____

Fact and Opinion: Henrietta

Directions: Read the story. Then, follow the instructions.

My name is Henrietta, and I am a humpback whale. I live in cold seas in the summer and warm seas in the winter. My long flippers are used to move forward and backward. I like to eat fish. Sometimes, I show off by leaping out of the water. Would you like to be a humpback whale?

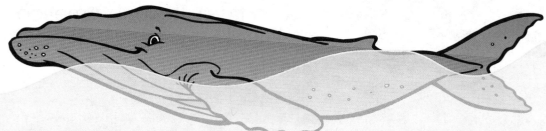

Write **F** next to each fact and **O** next to each opinion.

___O___ 1. Being a humpback whale is fun.

___F___ 2. Humpback whales live in cold seas during the summer.

___O___ 3. Whales are fun to watch.

___F___ 4. Humpback whales use their flippers to move forward and backward.

___F___ 5. Henrietta is a great name for a whale.

___F___ 6. Leaping out of water would be hard.

___F___ 7. Humpback whales like to eat fish.

___F___ 8. Humpback whales show off by leaping out of the water.

Making Inferences: Ryan's Top

Directions: Read about Ryan's top. Then, follow the instructions.

Ryan got a new top. He wanted to place it where it would be safe. He asked his dad to put it up high. Where can his dad put the top?

1. Write where Ryan's dad can put the top. _____

_____

Draw a place Ryan's dad can put the top.

Name _____

Making Inferences: Ant Farms

Directions: Read about ant farms. Then, answer the questions.

Ants are busy on the farm. They dig in the sand. They make roads in the sand. They look for food in the sand. When an ant dies, other ants bury it.

1. Where do you think ants are buried? <u>under</u>

   <u>ground</u>

2. Is it fair to say ants are lazy? <u>Of cours not</u>

3. Write a word that tells about ants. <u>There is an</u>
   <u>ant calld Bull Dog ant</u>

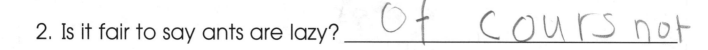

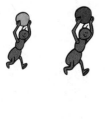     

Your Total Solution for Second Grade

Making Inferences

Directions: Read the story. Then, answer the questions.

Jeff is baking cookies. He wears special clothes when he bakes. He puts (flour, sugar, eggs,) and (butter) into a bowl. He mixes everything together. He puts the cookies in the oven at 11:15 A.M. It takes 15 minutes for the cookes to bake. Jeff wants something cold and white to drink when he eats his cookies.

1. Is Jeff baking a cake?   Yes No

2. What are two things Jeff might wear when he bakes?
   hat   boots   apron   tie   raincoat   roller skates

3. What didn't Jeff put in the cookies?
   flour   eggs   m~~il~~k   butter   sugar

4. What do you think Jeff does after he mixes the cookies but before he bakes them? _geos away and sarts to wave his ham_

5. What time will the cookies be done? _____

6. What will Jeff drink with his cookies? _____

7. ~~Why do you think Jeff~~ wanted to bake cookies? _____

_____

_____

Name _____

Making Inferences

Directions: Read the story. Then, answer the questions.

Mrs. Sweet looked forward to a visit from her niece, Candy. In the morning, she cleaned her house. She also baked a cherry pie. An hour before Candy was to arrive, the phone rang. Mrs. Sweet said, "I understand." When she hung up the phone, she looked very sad.

1. Who do you think called Mrs. Sweet?

   I think candy called
   Mrs. Sweet.

2. How do you know that?

   ~~because,~~   _unable to_
   answer

3. Why is Mrs. Sweet sad?

   _____

   _____

Your Total Solution for Second Grade

Making Inferences: Using Pictures

Directions: Draw a picture for each idea. Then, write two sentences that tell about it.

You and a friend are playing your favorite game.

_____

_____

You and a friend are sharing your favorite food.

_____

_____

Name _____

Making Inferences: Problem-Solving

Juniper has three problems to solve. She needs your help.

Directions: Read each problem. Write what you think she should do.

1. Juniper is watching her favorite TV show when the power goes out.

_____

_____

_____

_____

2. Juniper is riding her bike to school when the front tire goes flat.

_____

_____

_____

_____

3. Juniper loses her father while shopping in the supermarket.

_____

_____

_____

_____

Your Total Solution for Second Grade

Making Inferences: Writing Questions

Tommy likes to answer questions. He knows the answers, but you need to write the questions.

Directions: Write two questions for each answer.

Answer: It has four legs.

1. _____ cat _____ ?

_____ dog _____ ?

Answer: It lives on a farm.

2. _____ Pig _____ ?

_____ horse _____ ?

Answer: It is soft.

3. _____ cat _____ ?

_____ blanket _____ ?

Name _____

Making Inferences: Writing Questions

Toban and Sean use many colors when they paint.

Directions: Write two questions for each answer.

Answer: It is red.

1. ___what color did they use?_____ ?

_____ ?

Answer: It is purple.

2. _____ ?

_____ ?

Answer: It is green.

3. _____ ?

_____ ?

Your Total Solution for Second Grade

Making Inferences: Point of View

Chelsea likes to pretend she will meet famous people someday. She would like to ask them many questions.

Directions: Write a question you think Chelsea would ask if she met these people.

1. an actor in a popular, new film _____

_____ ?

2. an Olympic gold medal winner _____

_____ ?

3. an alien from outer space _____

_____ ?

Directions: Now, write the answers these people might have given to Chelsea's questions.

4. an actor in a popular, new film _____

_____

5. an Olympic gold medal winner _____

_____

6. an alien from outer space _____

_____

Name _____

Making Inferences: Point of View

Ellen likes animals. Someday, she might want to be an animal doctor.

Directions: Write one question you think Ellen would ask each of these animals if she could speak their language.

1. a giraffe _____ ?

2. a mouse _____ ?

3. a shark _____ ?

4. a hippopotamus _____ ?

5. a penguin _____ ?

6. a gorilla _____ ?

7. an eagle _____ ?

Directions: Now, write the answers you think these animals might have given Ellen.

8. a giraffe _____

9. a mouse _____

10. a shark _____

11. a hippopotamus _____

12. a penguin _____

13. a gorilla _____

14. an eagle _____

Your Total Solution for Second Grade

Name _____

Making Deductions: Find the Books

Directions: Use the clues to help the children find their books. Draw a line from each child's name to the correct book.

Brett   Aki   Lorenzo   Kate   Zac   Oralia

CHILDREN	BOOKS
Brett	jokes
Aki	cakes
Lorenzo	monsters
Kate	games
Zac	flags
Oralia	space

Clues

1. Lorenzo likes jokes.

2. Kate likes to bake.

3. Oralia likes far away places.

4. Aki does not like monsters or flags.

5. Zac does not like space or monsters.

6. Brett does not like games, jokes, or cakes.

Name _____

Making Deductions: Sports

Children all over the world like to play sports. They like many different kinds of sports: football, soccer, basketball, softball, in-line skating, swimming, and more.

Directions: Read the clues. Draw dots and **X**s on the chart to match the children with their sports.

	swimming	football	soccer	basketball	baseball	in-line skating
J.J.						
Zoe						
Andy						
Amber						
Raul						
Sierra						

Clues
1. Zoe hates football.
2. Andy likes basketball.
3. Raul likes to pitch in his favorite sport.
4. J.J. likes to play what Zoe hates.
5. Amber is good at kicking the ball to her teammates.
6. Sierra needs a pool for her favorite sport.

Your Total Solution for Second Grade

Fiction/Nonfiction: The Fourth of July

Directions: Read each story. Then, write whether it is fiction or nonfiction.

One sunny day in July, a dog named Stan ran away from home. He went up one street and down the other looking for fun, but all the yards were empty. Where was everybody? Stan kept walking until he heard the sound of band music and happy people. Stan walked faster until he got to Central Street. There he saw men, women, children, and dogs getting ready to walk in a parade. It was the Fourth of July!

Fiction or Nonfiction?_____

Americans celebrate the Fourth of July every year, because it is the birthday of the United States of America. On July 4, 1776, the United States got its independence from Great Britain. Today, Americans celebrate this holiday with parades, picnics, and fireworks as they proudly wave the red, white, and blue American flag.

Fiction or Nonfiction?_____

Name _____

Fiction and Nonfiction: Which Is It?

Directions: Read about fiction and nonfiction books. Then, follow the instructions.

There are many kinds of books. Some books have make-believe stories about princesses and dragons. Some books contain poetry and rhymes, like Mother Goose. These are fiction.

Some books contain facts about space and plants. And still other books have stories about famous people in history like Abraham Lincoln. These are nonfiction.

Write **F** for fiction and **NF** for nonfiction.

_____ 1. nursery rhyme

_____ 2. fairy tale

_____ 3. true life story of a famous athlete

_____ 4. Aesop's fables

_____ 5. dictionary entry about foxes

_____ 6. weather report

_____ 7. story about a talking tree

_____ 8. story about how a tadpole becomes a frog

_____ 9. story about animal habitats

_____ 10. riddles and jokes

Your Total Solution for Second Grade

MATH

Name _____

Counting by Twos

Directions: Each basket the players make is worth 2 points. Help your team win by counting by twos to beat the other team's score.

2

4

6

8

___

10

12

16

18

20

22

24

26

28

30

32

Winner!

yay!

34

Final Score	
Home	**Visitor**
☐	**30**

Your Total Solution for Second Grade

Counting: Twos, Fives, Tens

Directions: Write the missing numbers.

Count by twos:

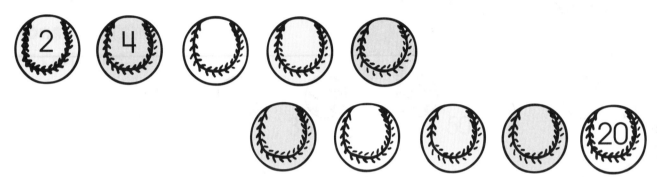

Count by fives:

Count by tens:

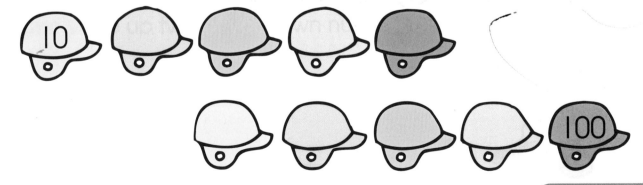

Name _____

Finding Patterns: Shapes

Directions: Complete each row by drawing the correct shape.

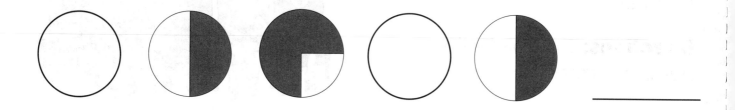

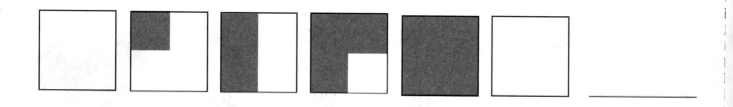

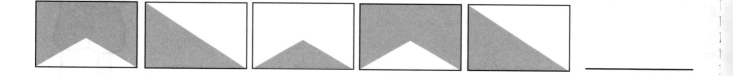

Your Total Solution for Second Grade

Ordinal Numbers

Ordinal numbers indicate order in a series, such as **first**, **second**, or **third**.

Directions: Follow the instructions to color the train cars. The first car is the engine.

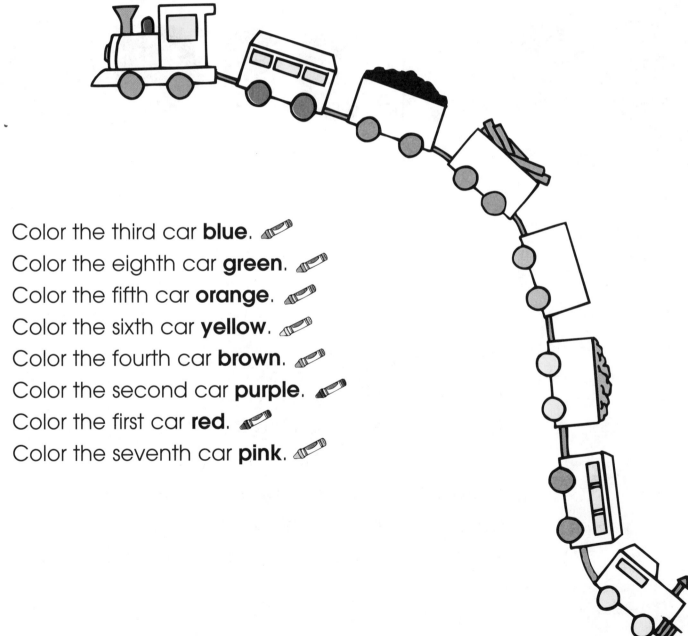

Color the third car **blue**.
Color the eighth car **green**.
Color the fifth car **orange**.
Color the sixth car **yellow**.
Color the fourth car **brown**.
Color the second car **purple**.
Color the first car **red**.
Color the seventh car **pink**.

Name _____

Ordinal Numbers

Directions: Follow the instructions.

Draw glasses on the second one.

Put a hat on the fourth one.

Color blonde hair on the third one.

Draw a tie on the first one.

Draw ears on the fifth one.

Draw black hair on the seventh one.

Put a bow on the head of the sixth one.

Your Total Solution for Second Grade

Addition

Addition is "putting together" or adding two or more numbers to find the sum.

Directions: Add.

Example:

```
   2
 + 5
 ———
   7
```

3 + 4	6 + 2	7 + 1	8 + 2	5 + 4	3 + 1
8 + 2	9 + 5	10 + 3	6 + 6	4 + 9	7 + 7
9 + 3	8 + 7	6 + 5	7 + 9	7 + 6	9 + 9

Addition: Commutative Property

The commutative property of addition states that even if the order of the numbers is changed in an addition sentence, the sum will stay the same.

Example: 2 + 3 = 5
           3 + 2 = 5

Directions: Look at the addition sentences below. Complete the addition sentences by writing the missing numerals.

5 + 4 = 9	3 + 1 = 4	2 + 6 = 8
4 + __ = 9	1 + __ = 4	6 + __ = 8

6 + 1 = 7	4 + 3 = 7	1 + 9 = 10
1 + __ = 7	3 + __ = 7	9 + __ = 10

Now try these:

6 + 3 = 9	10 + 2 = 12	8 + 3 = 11
__ + __ = 9	__ + __ = 12	__ + __ = 11

Look at these sums. Can you think of two number sentences that would show the commutative property of addition?

__ + __ = 7	__ + __ = 11	__ + __ = 9
__ + __ = 7	__ + __ = 11	__ + __ = 9

Your Total Solution for Second Grade

Adding Three or More Numbers

Directions: Add all the numbers to find the sum. Draw pictures to help or break up the problem into two smaller problems.

Example:

$$\begin{array}{r} 1 \\ 2 \\ +3 \\ \hline 6 \end{array}$$ ○ ○○ ○○○

$$\begin{array}{r} 2 \\ +5 \\ \end{array}$$ ⟩ 7 $$\begin{array}{r} 2 \\ +4 \\ \hline \end{array}$$ ⟩ $$\begin{array}{r} +6 \\ \hline 13 \end{array}$$

$$\begin{array}{r} 3 \\ 6 \\ +2 \\ \hline 11 \end{array}$$
$$\begin{array}{r} 8 \\ 5 \\ +4 \\ \hline 17 \end{array}$$
$$\begin{array}{r} 3 \\ 1 \\ +5 \\ \hline 9 \end{array}$$
$$\begin{array}{r} 8 \\ 2 \\ +9 \\ \hline 19 \end{array}$$

$$\begin{array}{r} 2 \\ 8 \\ 4 \\ +3 \\ \hline 17 \end{array}$$
$$\begin{array}{r} 3 \\ 6 \\ 5 \\ +2 \\ \hline \end{array}$$
$$\begin{array}{r} 4 \\ 1 \\ 2 \\ +5 \\ \hline \end{array}$$
$$\begin{array}{r} 6 \\ 7 \\ 3 \\ +1 \\ \hline \end{array}$$

Name _____

Two-Digit Addition

Directions: Study the example. Follow the steps to add.

Example:

$$\begin{array}{r} 33 \\ +41 \end{array}$$

Step 1: Add the ones.

tens	ones
3	3
+ 4	1
	4

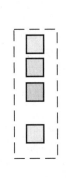

Step 2: Add the tens.

tens	ones
3	3
+ 4	1
7	4

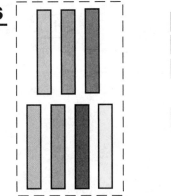

tens	ones
4	2
+ 2	4
6	6

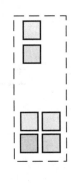

tens	ones
5	0
+ 4	7
9	7

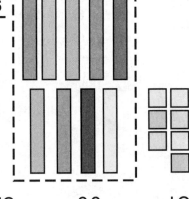

$$\begin{array}{r} 24 \\ +62 \end{array} \qquad \begin{array}{r} 15 \\ +23 \end{array} \qquad \begin{array}{r} 38 \\ +61 \end{array} \qquad \begin{array}{r} 11 \\ +26 \end{array} \qquad \begin{array}{r} 37 \\ +42 \end{array} \qquad \begin{array}{r} 72 \\ +11 \end{array} \qquad \begin{array}{r} 33 \\ +51 \end{array} \qquad \begin{array}{r} 10 \\ +30 \end{array}$$

$$\begin{array}{r} 25 \\ +42 \end{array} \qquad \begin{array}{r} 62 \\ +14 \end{array} \qquad \begin{array}{r} 32 \\ +44 \end{array} \qquad \begin{array}{r} 25 \\ +13 \end{array} \qquad \begin{array}{r} 82 \\ + 6 \end{array} \qquad \begin{array}{r} 91 \\ + 5 \end{array} \qquad \begin{array}{r} 16 \\ +71 \end{array} \qquad \begin{array}{r} 55 \\ + 3 \end{array}$$

Your Total Solution for Second Grade

Two-Digit Addition

Directions: Add the total points scored in each game. Remember to add **ones** first and **tens** second.

Example:

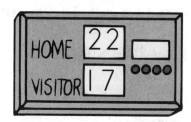

Total ___39___

Total _____

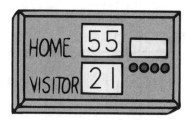

Total _____

Total _____

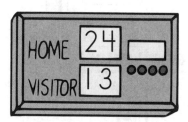

Total _____

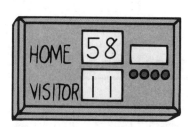

Total _____

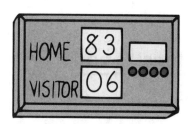

Total _____

Total _____

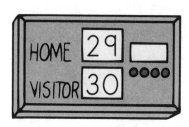

Total _____

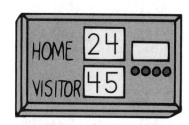

Total _____

Name _____

Two-Digit Addition: Regrouping

Addition is "putting together" or adding two or more numbers to find the sum. Regrouping is using **ten ones** to form **one ten**, **ten tens** to form **one 100**, **fifteen ones** to form **one ten** and **five ones**, and so on.

Directions: Study the examples. Follow the steps to add.

Example:
$$\begin{array}{r} 14 \\ +\ 8 \\ \hline \end{array}$$

Step 1: Add the ones.

tens	ones
1	4
+	8
	12

Step 2: Regroup the tens.

tens	ones
1	4
+	8
	2

Step 3: Add the tens.

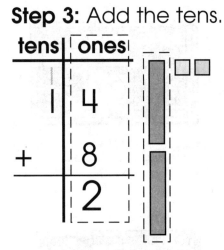

tens	ones
1	4
+	8
	2

tens	ones
1	6
+ 3	7
5	3

tens	ones
3	8
+ 5	3
9	1

tens	ones
2	4
+ 4	7
7	1

$$\begin{array}{r} 34 \\ +17 \\ \hline \end{array} \qquad \begin{array}{r} 23 \\ +38 \\ \hline \end{array} \qquad \begin{array}{r} 25 \\ +25 \\ \hline \end{array} \qquad \begin{array}{r} 16 \\ +55 \\ \hline \end{array} \qquad \begin{array}{r} 39 \\ +48 \\ \hline \end{array} \qquad \begin{array}{r} 19 \\ +64 \\ \hline \end{array} \qquad \begin{array}{r} 58 \\ +33 \\ \hline \end{array} \qquad \begin{array}{r} 16 \\ +15 \\ \hline \end{array}$$

Your Total Solution for Second Grade

Two-Digit Addition: Regrouping

Directions: Add the total points scored in the game. Remember to add the ones, regroup, and then add the tens.

Example:

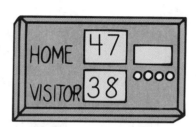

Total _85_

Total _____

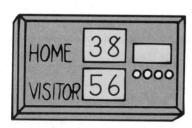

Total _____

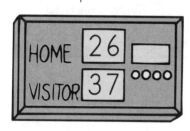

Total _____

Total _____

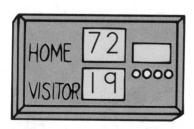

Total _____

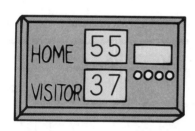

Total _____

Total _____

Total _____

Total _____

Name _____

Three-Digit Addition: Regrouping

Directions: Study the examples. Follow the steps to add.

Example:

Step 1: Add the ones.

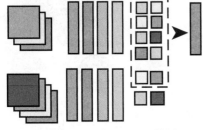

Do you regroup? Yes

Step 2: Add the tens.

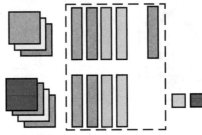

Do you regroup? No

Step 3: Add the hundreds.

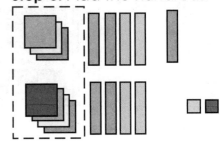

hundreds	tens	ones	hundreds	tens	ones	hundreds	tens	ones
	1			1			1	
3	4	8	3	4	8	3	4	8
+ 4	4	4	+ 4	4	4	+ 4	4	4
		2		9	2	7	9	2

hundreds	tens	ones	hundreds	tens	ones	hundreds	tens	ones
	1			1			1	
2	1	4	3	6	8	1	1	9
+ 2	3	8	+ 2	1	3	+ 5	6	5
4	5	2		8	1			4

418	471	334	659	736	426	567	327
+ 323	+ 319	+ 528	+ 127	+ 145	+ 165	+ 228	+ 354

Your Total Solution for Second Grade

Three-Digit Addition: Regrouping

Directions: Study the example. Follow the steps to add. Regroup when needed.

Step 1: Add the ones.
Step 2: Add the tens.
Step 3: Add the hundreds.

hundreds	tens	ones
1	1	
3	4	8
+ 4	5	4
8	0	2

$$
\begin{array}{r} 348 \\ + 214 \\ \hline \end{array}
\qquad
\begin{array}{r} 172 \\ + 418 \\ \hline \end{array}
\qquad
\begin{array}{r} 575 \\ + 329 \\ \hline \end{array}
\qquad
\begin{array}{r} 623 \\ + 268 \\ \hline \end{array}
\qquad
\begin{array}{r} 369 \\ + 533 \\ \hline \end{array}
\qquad
\begin{array}{r} 733 \\ + 229 \\ \hline \end{array}
$$

$$
\begin{array}{r} 411 \\ + 299 \\ \hline \end{array}
\qquad
\begin{array}{r} 423 \\ + 169 \\ \hline \end{array}
\qquad
\begin{array}{r} 639 \\ + 177 \\ \hline \end{array}
\qquad
\begin{array}{r} 624 \\ + 368 \\ \hline \end{array}
\qquad
\begin{array}{r} 272 \\ + 469 \\ \hline \end{array}
\qquad
\begin{array}{r} 393 \\ + 418 \\ \hline \end{array}
$$

Subtraction

Subtraction is "taking away" or subtracting one number from another to find the difference.

Directions: Subtract.

Example:

$$\begin{array}{r} 4 \\ -\,3 \\ \hline 1 \end{array}$$

$$\begin{array}{r} 5 \\ -\,3 \\ \hline 2 \end{array} \qquad \begin{array}{r} 6 \\ -\,1 \\ \hline 5 \end{array} \qquad \begin{array}{r} 4 \\ -\,3 \\ \hline 1 \end{array} \qquad \begin{array}{r} 3 \\ -\,1 \\ \hline 2 \end{array} \qquad \begin{array}{r} 2 \\ -\,0 \\ \hline 2 \end{array} \qquad \begin{array}{r} 1 \\ -\,1 \\ \hline 0 \end{array}$$

$$\begin{array}{r} 9 \\ -\,2 \\ \hline 7 \end{array} \qquad \begin{array}{r} 7 \\ -\,4 \\ \hline 3 \end{array} \qquad \begin{array}{r} 10 \\ -\,5 \\ \hline 5 \end{array} \qquad \begin{array}{r} 14 \\ -\,6 \\ \hline 8 \end{array} \qquad \begin{array}{r} 15 \\ -\,9 \\ \hline 6 \end{array} \qquad \begin{array}{r} 12 \\ -\,3 \\ \hline 9 \end{array}$$

$$\begin{array}{r} 18 \\ -\,8 \\ \hline 10 \end{array} \qquad \begin{array}{r} 13 \\ -\,5 \\ \hline 8 \end{array} \qquad \begin{array}{r} 14 \\ -\,7 \\ \hline 7 \end{array} \qquad \begin{array}{r} 11 \\ -\,4 \\ \hline 7 \end{array} \qquad \begin{array}{r} 17 \\ -\,9 \\ \hline 8 \end{array} \qquad \begin{array}{r} 16 \\ -\,8 \\ \hline 8 \end{array}$$

Your Total Solution for Second Grade

Two-Digit Subtraction

Directions: Study the example. Follow the steps to subtract.

Example:
$$\begin{array}{r} 28 \\ -14 \\ \hline \end{array}$$

Step 1: Subtract the ones.

tens	ones
2	8
– 1	4
	4

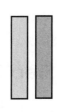 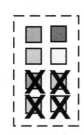

Step 2: Subtract the tens.

tens	ones
2	8
– 1	4
1	4

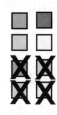

tens	ones
2	4
– 1	2
1	2

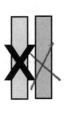

tens	ones
3	8
– 1	5
2	3

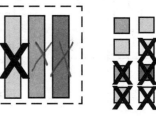

$$\begin{array}{r} 24 \\ -12 \\ \hline 12 \end{array} \quad \begin{array}{r} 61 \\ -30 \\ \hline 31 \end{array} \quad \begin{array}{r} 77 \\ -44 \\ \hline 33 \end{array} \quad \begin{array}{r} 85 \\ -24 \\ \hline 61 \end{array} \quad \begin{array}{r} 57 \\ -23 \\ \hline 34 \end{array} \quad \begin{array}{r} 87 \\ -33 \\ \hline 54 \end{array} \quad \begin{array}{r} 59 \\ -34 \\ \hline 25 \end{array} \quad \begin{array}{r} 96 \\ -16 \\ \hline 80 \end{array}$$

$$\begin{array}{r} 29 \\ -15 \\ \hline 14 \end{array} \quad \begin{array}{r} 74 \\ -51 \\ \hline 23 \end{array} \quad \begin{array}{r} 46 \\ -32 \\ \hline 14 \end{array} \quad \begin{array}{r} 69 \\ -35 \\ \hline 34 \end{array} \quad \begin{array}{r} 95 \\ -32 \\ \hline \end{array} \quad \begin{array}{r} 33 \\ -33 \\ \hline \end{array} \quad \begin{array}{r} 78 \\ -26 \\ \hline \end{array} \quad \begin{array}{r} 22 \\ -11 \\ \hline \end{array}$$

Name _____

Two-Digit Subtraction: Regrouping

Subtraction is "taking away" or subtracting one number from another to find the difference. Regrouping is using **one ten** to form **ten ones**, **one 100** to form **ten tens**, and so on.

Directions: Study the examples. Follow the steps to subtract.

Example:
$$\begin{array}{r} 37 \\ -19 \\ \hline \end{array}$$

Step 1: Regroup.

Step 2: Subtract the ones.

Step 3: Subtract the tens.

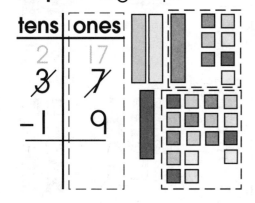

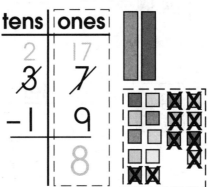

tens	ones
0	12
X̶	2
-	9
	3

tens	ones
2	14
3̶	4̶
-1	6
1	8

tens	ones
3	15
4̶	5̶
-2	9
1	6

$$\begin{array}{r} 48 \\ -19 \\ \hline \end{array} \qquad \begin{array}{r} 33 \\ -18 \\ \hline \end{array} \qquad \begin{array}{r} 14 \\ -\ 8 \\ \hline \end{array} \qquad \begin{array}{r} 40 \\ -12 \\ \hline \end{array} \qquad \begin{array}{r} 41 \\ -25 \\ \hline \end{array} \qquad \begin{array}{r} 63 \\ -35 \\ \hline \end{array} \qquad \begin{array}{r} 32 \\ -13 \\ \hline \end{array} \qquad \begin{array}{r} 54 \\ -25 \\ \hline \end{array}$$

Your Total Solution for Second Grade

Name _____

Two-Digit Subtraction: Regrouping

Directions: Study the steps for subtracting. Solve the problems using the steps.

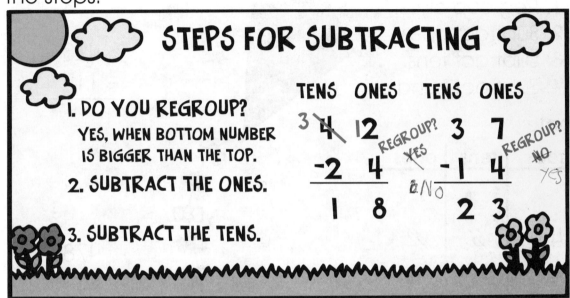

STEPS FOR SUBTRACTING

1. DO YOU REGROUP?
   YES, WHEN BOTTOM NUMBER IS BIGGER THAN THE TOP.
2. SUBTRACT THE ONES.
3. SUBTRACT THE TENS.

TENS	ONES		TENS	ONES
³4̸	12		3	7
-2	4		-1	4
1	8		2	3

REGROUP? YES & No   REGROUP? No Yes

tens	ones
4	7
- 2	8

tens	ones
6	4
- 3	4

tens	ones
5	3
- 3	9

56	83	43	75	91
- 38	- 19	- 26	- 27	- 82
18	64	17	48	009

73	35	67	26	68
- 44	- 17	- 28	- 18	- 29

Name _____

Three-Digit Subtraction: Regrouping

Directions: Study the example. Follow the steps to subtract.

Step 1: Regroup ones.
Step 2: Subtract ones.
Step 3: Subtract tens.
Step 4: Subtract hundreds.

Example:

hundreds	tens	ones
	5	12
4	6̸	2̸
− 2	5	3
2	0	9

$$
\begin{array}{r} 423 \\ -\,114 \\ \hline \end{array}
\qquad
\begin{array}{r} 562 \\ -\,349 \\ \hline \end{array}
$$

$$
\begin{array}{r} 478 \\ -\,239 \\ \hline \end{array}
\qquad
\begin{array}{r} 651 \\ -\,333 \\ \hline \end{array}
$$

Directions: Draw a line to the correct answer. Color the kites.

$$
\begin{array}{r} 347 \\ -\,218 \\ \hline \end{array}
\quad
\begin{array}{r} 144 \\ -\,135 \\ \hline \end{array}
\quad
\begin{array}{r} 963 \\ -\,748 \\ \hline \end{array}
\quad
\begin{array}{r} 762 \\ -\,553 \\ \hline \end{array}
\quad
\begin{array}{r} 287 \\ -\,179 \\ \hline \end{array}
\quad
\begin{array}{r} 427 \\ -\,398 \\ \hline \end{array}
$$

089

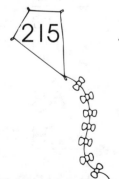
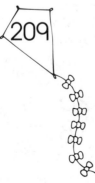
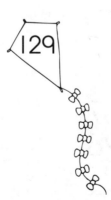
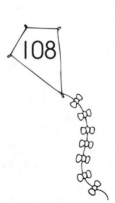
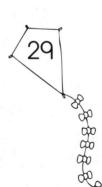
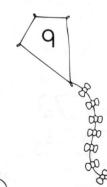

215   209   129   108   29   9

Your Total Solution for Second Grade

Three-Digit Subtraction: Regrouping

Directions: Subtract. Circle the **7**s that appear in the **tens place**.

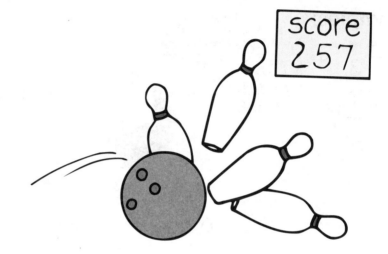

score
257

$$\begin{array}{r} 492 \\ -\ 221 \\ \hline 271 \end{array}$$

$$\begin{array}{r} 184 \\ -\ 129 \\ \hline \end{array}$$

$$\begin{array}{r} 358 \\ -\ 238 \\ \hline \end{array}$$

$$\begin{array}{r} 765 \\ -\ 326 \\ \hline \end{array}$$

$$\begin{array}{r} 584 \\ -\ 435 \\ \hline \end{array}$$

$$\begin{array}{r} 693 \\ -\ 314 \\ \hline \end{array}$$

$$\begin{array}{r} 921 \\ -\ 362 \\ \hline \end{array}$$

$$\begin{array}{r} 128 \\ -\ 109 \\ \hline \end{array}$$

$$\begin{array}{r} 744 \\ -\ 674 \\ \hline \end{array}$$

$$\begin{array}{r} 835 \\ -\ 217 \\ \hline \end{array}$$

$$\begin{array}{r} 248 \\ -\ 199 \\ \hline \end{array}$$

$$\begin{array}{r} 635 \\ -\ 428 \\ \hline \end{array}$$

Name _____

Addition and Subtraction

Directions: Add or subtract. Circle the answers that are less than 10.

Examples:

3
+ 1
─────
4

3
− 1
─────
2

9 + 3	6 − 2	12 − 1	18 + 1	15 − 6
7 + 6	16 − 9	10 − 3	14 + 5	16 − 8
8 + 7	12 + 2	13 − 4	17 + 2	9 + 9

Your Total Solution for Second Grade

Review

Name _____

Directions: Add or subtract. Use regrouping when needed. Always do ones first and tens last.

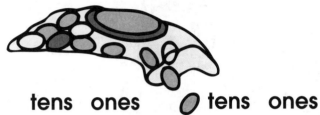

tens	ones		tens	ones		tens	ones		tens	ones
9	3		3	0		6	5		7	1
- 2	5		+ 2	7		+ 1	7		- 3	6

57

tens	ones		tens	ones		tens	ones		tens	ones
7	6		8	2		5	6		2	5
- 2	8		+ 1	9		- 2	8		- 1	6

2 8

tens	ones		tens	ones		tens	ones		tens	ones
4	3		5	3		2	4		4	8
- 1	4		- 1	5		+ 5	7		+ 2	8

33	52	46	97
+ 47	+ 29	- 37	- 68

Name _____

Two-Digit Addition and Subtraction

Directions: Add or subtract using regrouping.

Example:

```
   tens  ones
    2    15
    ȝ     5
   -2     7
   ─────────
          8
```

```
  56     40     35     42     53     97     44     93
- 27   - 16   + 27   - 14   + 38   - 48   + 27   - 39
```

```
  56     44     68     73     33     49     77     27
- 17   + 28   + 49   - 24   + 18   + 32   - 68   + 19
```

Your Total Solution for Second Grade

Two-Digit Addition and Subtraction

Directions: Add or subtract using regrouping.

```
  23          84          69          41
+ 48        - 56        + 29        - 17
____        ____        ____        ____


  52          73          84          57
- 28        + 18        - 27        - 39
____        ____        ____        ____


  33          64          37          36
- 15        + 17        + 58        - 19
____        ____        ____        ____


  65          48          33          25
- 28        - 30        + 18        + 35
____        ____        ____        ____
```

Problem-Solving

Directions: Tell whether you should add or subtract. "In all" is a clue to add. "Left" is a clue to subtract. Draw pictures to help you.

Example:

Jane's dog has 5 bones. He ate 3 bones. How many bones are left?

subtract
_____

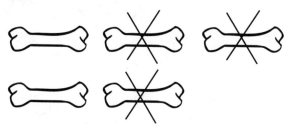

$$\begin{array}{r} 5 \\ \boxed{} - 3 \\ \hline 2 \end{array}$$ bones

Lucky the cat had 5 mice. She got 4 more for her birthday. How many mice did she have in all?

_____

☐

_____ mice

Sam bought 6 fish. She gave 2 fish to a friend. How many fish does she have left?

_____

☐

_____ fish

Place Value: Ones, Tens

The place value of a digit or numeral is shown by where it is in the number. For example, in the number **23**, **2** has the place value of **tens**, and **3** is **ones**.

Directions: Add the tens and ones and write your answers in the blanks.

Example:

3 tens   +   3 ones = __33__

                                                                      = __33__

tens ones	tens ones
8 tens + 5 ones = _____	6 tens + 0 ones = _____
7 tens + 3 ones = _____	8 tens + 1 one = _____
3 tens + 2 ones = _____	1 ten + 1 one = _____
5 tens + 4 ones = _____	4 tens + 3 ones = _____
9 tens + 5 ones = _____	

Directions: Draw a line to the correct number.

6 tens + 7 ones	73
4 tens + 2 ones	67
8 tens + 0 ones	51
7 tens + 3 ones	80
5 tens + 1 one	42

Place Value: Ones, Tens

Directions: Write the numbers for the tens and ones. Then, add.

Example:

2 tens + 7 ones

20 + 7

27

4 tens + 2 ones

___ + ___

___

2 tens + 4 ones

___ + ___

___

9 tens + 3 ones

___ + ___

___

6 tens + 8 ones

___ + ___

___

Your Total Solution for Second Grade

Place Value: Hundreds

The place value of a digit or numeral is shown by where it is in the number. For example, in the number **123**, **1** has the place value of **hundreds**, **2** is **tens**, and **3** is **ones**.

Directions: Study the examples. Then, write the missing numbers in the blanks.

Examples:

2 hundreds + 3 tens + 6 ones =   1 hundred + 4 tens + 9 ones =

hundreds	tens	ones
2	3	6

= _236_

hundreds	tens	ones
1	4	9

= _149_

	hundreds	tens	ones	total
3 hundreds + 4 tens + 8 ones =	3	4	8	= _____
_ hundreds + _ ten + _ ones =	2	1	7	= _____
_ hundreds + _ tens + _ ones =	6	3	5	= _____
_ hundreds + _ tens + _ ones =	4	7	9	= _____
_ hundreds + _ tens + _ ones =	2	9	4	= _____
_ hundreds + 5 tens + 6 ones =	4	___	___	= _____
3 hundreds + 1 ten + 3 ones =	___	___	___	= _____
3 hundreds + _ tens + 7 ones =	___	5	___	= _____
6 hundreds + 2 tens + _ ones =	___	___	8	= _____

Name _____

Place Value: **Hundreds**

Directions: Write the numbers for hundreds, tens, and ones.
Then, add.

Example:

1 hundred + 4 tens + 6 ones
100 + 40 + 6
146

7 hundreds + 3 tens + 5 ones
____ + ____ + ____
____

3 hundreds + 1 ten + 9 ones
____ + ____ + ____
____

5 hundreds + 8 tens + 0 ones
____ + ____ + ____
____

9 hundreds + 0 tens + 7 ones
____ + ____ + ____
____

Your Total Solution for Second Grade

Graphs

Directions: Count the bananas in each row. Color the boxes to show how many have been eaten by the monkeys.

Name _____

Graphs

Directions: Count the fish. Color the bowls to make a graph that shows the number of fish.

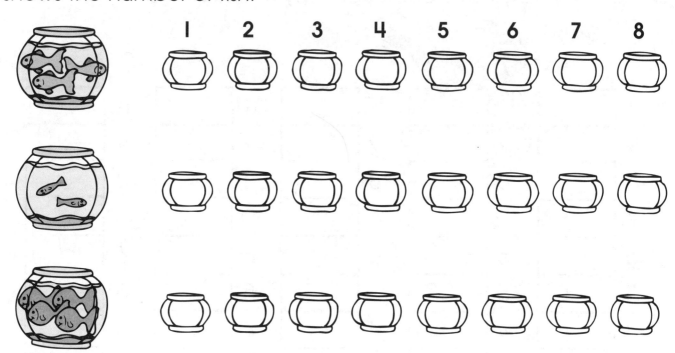

Directions: Use your fishbowl graphs to find the answers to the following questions. Draw a line to the correct bowl.

The most fish

The fewest fish

Your Total Solution for Second Grade

Multiplication

Multiplication is a short way to find the sum of adding the same number a certain amount of times. For example, **4 x 7 = 28** instead of **7 + 7 + 7 + 7 = 28**.

Directions: Study the example. Solve the problems.

Example:

3 + 3 + 3 = 9
3 threes = 9
3 x 3 = 9

7 + 7 = __14__
2 sevens = __14__
2 x 7 = __14__

4 + 4 + 4 + 4 = _____
4 fours = _____
4 x _____ = _____

5 + 5 = _____
2 fives = _____
2 x _____ = _____

2 + 2 + 2 + 2 = _____
4 twos = _____
4 x _____ = _____

6 + 6 = _____
2 sixes = _____
2 x _____ = _____

Multiplication

Directions: Draw a picture for each problem.
Then, write the missing numbers.

Example:

Draw 2 groups of three bugs.

$$3 + 3 = 6$$
$$\text{or} \quad 2 \times 3 = 6$$

Draw 3 groups of four hearts.	Draw 2 groups of five boxes.

$4 + 4 + 4 = \underline{12}$ or $\quad 3 \times \underline{4} = \underline{12}$	$5 + \underline{\quad} = \underline{\quad}$ or $\quad 2 \times \underline{\quad} = \underline{\quad}$

Draw 6 groups of two circles.

$$2 + \underline{\quad} + \underline{\quad} + \underline{\quad} + \underline{\quad} + \underline{\quad} = \underline{\quad}$$
$$\text{or} \quad 6 \times \underline{\quad} = \underline{\quad}$$

Draw 7 groups of three triangles.

$$3 + \underline{3} + \underline{3} + \underline{3} + \underline{3} + 3 + \underline{3} = \underline{3}$$
$$\text{or} \quad \underline{\quad} \times \underline{\quad} = \underline{\quad}$$

Multiplication

Directions: Study the example. Draw the groups and write the total.

Example:

3 x 2
2 + 2 + 2 = 6 ____

●● ●● ●●

3 x 4

___ + ___ + ___ = _____

2 x 5

___ + ___ = _____

5 x 3

___ + ___ + ___ + ___ + ___ = _____

Name _____

Multiplication

Directions: Solve the problems.

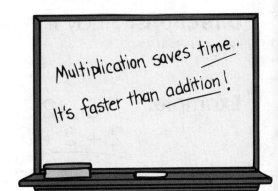

Multiplication saves time.
It's faster than addition!

9 + 9 = __18__   7 + 7 = ____

2 nines = ____   2 sevens = ____

2 x 9 = ____   2 x __7__ = ____

4 + 4 + 4 + 4 = ____   8 + 8 + 8 + 8 + 8 = ____

__4__ fours = ____   ____ eights = ____

____ x 4 = ____   ____ x 8 = ____

5 + 5 + 5 = ____   9 + 9 = ____   6 + 6 + 6 = ____

____ fives = ____   ____ nines = ____   ____ sixes = ____

____ x 5 = ____   ____ x 9 = ____   ____ x 6 = ____

3 + 3 = ____   7 + 7 + 7 + 7 = ____   2 + 2 = ____

____ threes = ____   ____ sevens = ____   ____ twos = ____

____ x 3 = ____   ____ x 7 = ____   ____ x 2 = ____

Your Total Solution for Second Grade

Problem-Solving

Directions: Tell if you add, subtract, or multiply. Then, write the answer.

Example:
There were 12 frogs sitting on a log by a pond, but 3 frogs hopped away. How many frogs are left?

___Subtract___ ___9___ frogs

There are 9 flowers growing by the pond.
Each flower has 2 leaves.
How many leaves are there?

_____ _____ leaves

A tree had 7 squirrels playing in it.
Then, 8 more came along.
How many squirrels are there in all?

_____ _____ squirrels

There were 27 birds living in the trees around the pond, but 9 flew away.
How many birds are left?

_____ _____ birds

Name _____

Fractions: Half, Third, Fourth

A **fraction** is a number that names part of a whole, such as $\frac{1}{2}$ or $\frac{1}{3}$.

Directions: Study the examples. Color the correct fraction of each shape.

Examples:

shaded part 1
equal parts 2
$\frac{1}{2}$ (one-half) shaded

shaded part 1
equal parts 3
$\frac{1}{3}$ (one-third) shaded

shaded part 1
equal parts 4
$\frac{1}{4}$ (one-fourth) shaded

Color: $\frac{1}{3}$ red	
Color: $\frac{1}{4}$ blue	
Color: $\frac{1}{2}$ orange	

Your Total Solution for Second Grade

Fractions: Half, Third, Fourth

Directions: Study the examples. Circle the fraction that shows the shaded part. Then, circle the fraction that shows the white part.

Examples:

shaded　　white

$\frac{1}{4}$　$\frac{1}{3}$　$\boxed{\frac{1}{2}}$　　$\frac{1}{3}$　$\boxed{\frac{1}{2}}$　$\frac{1}{4}$

shaded　　white

$\frac{1}{2}$　$\boxed{\frac{2}{3}}$　$\frac{3}{4}$　　$\frac{2}{3}$　$\frac{1}{2}$　$\boxed{\frac{1}{3}}$

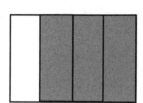

shaded　　white

$\frac{1}{4}$　$\frac{1}{2}$　$\boxed{\frac{3}{4}}$　　$\boxed{\frac{1}{4}}$　$\frac{2}{3}$　$\frac{1}{2}$

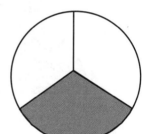

shaded　　　　white

$\frac{1}{4}$　$\frac{1}{3}$　$\frac{1}{2}$　　　$\frac{2}{4}$　$\frac{2}{3}$　$\frac{2}{2}$

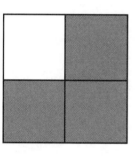

shaded　　　　white

$\frac{3}{4}$　$\frac{1}{3}$　$\frac{3}{2}$　　　$\frac{1}{2}$　$\frac{1}{4}$　$\frac{1}{3}$

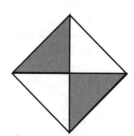

shaded　　　　white

$\frac{2}{3}$　$\frac{2}{4}$　$\frac{2}{2}$　　　$\frac{1}{3}$　$\frac{2}{4}$　$\frac{2}{2}$

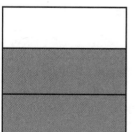

shaded　　　　white

$\frac{2}{4}$　$\frac{2}{3}$　$\frac{2}{2}$　　　$\frac{1}{2}$　$\frac{1}{4}$　$\frac{1}{3}$

Name _____

Fractions: Half, Third, Fourth

Directions: Draw a line from the fraction to the correct shape.

$\frac{1}{4}$ shaded

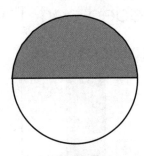

$\frac{2}{4}$ shaded

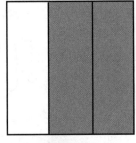

$\frac{1}{2}$ shaded

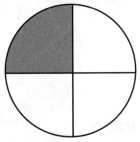

$\frac{1}{3}$ shaded

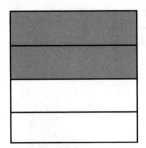

$\frac{2}{3}$ shaded

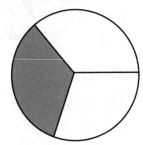

Your Total Solution for Second Grade

Problem-Solving: Fractions

Directions: Read each problem. Use the pictures to help you solve the problem. Write the fraction that answers the question.

Simon and Jessie shared a pizza.
Together they ate $\frac{3}{4}$ of the pizza.
How much of the pizza is left? _____

Sylvia baked a cherry pie. She gave $\frac{1}{3}$
to her grandmother and $\frac{1}{3}$ to a friend.
How much of the pie did she keep? _____

Timmy erased $\frac{1}{2}$ of the blackboard
before the bell rang for recess.
How much of the blackboard does
he have left to erase? _____

Directions: Read the problem. Draw your own picture to help you solve the problem. Write the fraction that answers the question.

Sarah mowed $\frac{1}{4}$ of the yard before lunch.
How much does she have left to mow? _____

Name _____

Geometry

Geometry is mathematics that has to do with lines and shapes.

Directions: Color the shapes.

Color the triangles **blue**.
Color the circles **red**.
Color the squares **green**.
Color the rectangles **pink**.

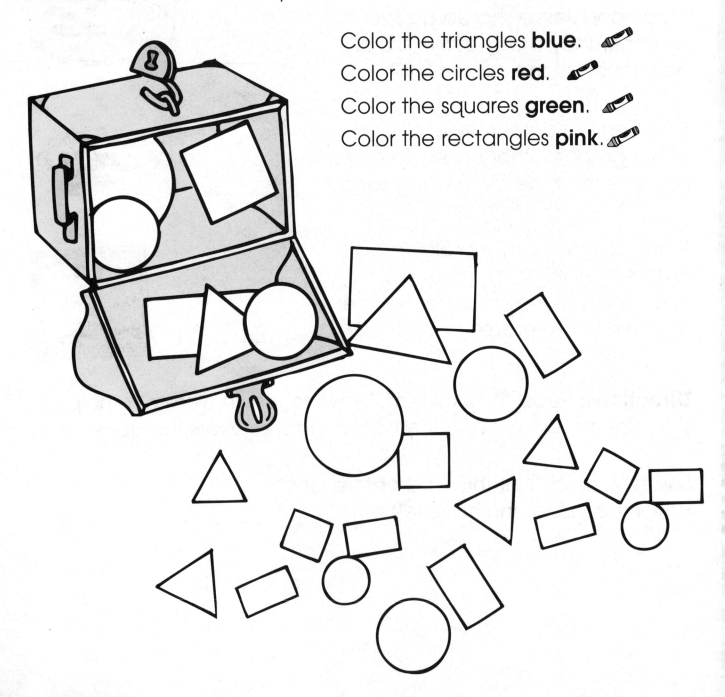

Your Total Solution for Second Grade

Geometry

Directions: Cut out the tangram below. Mix up the pieces. Try to put it back together into a square.

Geometry

Directions: Draw a line from the word to the shape.

Use a red line for circles.
Use a blue line for squares.
Use a yellow line for rectangles.
Use a green line for triangles.

Circle   **Square**   **Triangle**   **Rectangle**

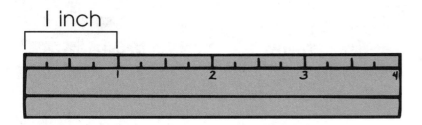
Measurement: Inches

An **inch** is a unit of length in the standard measurement system.

Directions: Use a ruler to measure each object to the nearest inch.

I inch

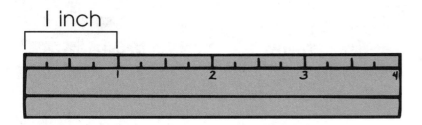

about __1__ inch

about _____ inch

about _____ inches

about _____ inches

about _____ inches

about _____ inches

about _____ inches

Your Total Solution for Second Grade

Measurement

Directions: Cut out the ruler. Measure each object to the nearest inch.

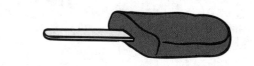

_____ inches

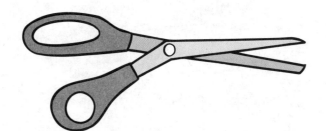

_____ inches

_____ inch

Directions: Measure objects around your house. Write the measurement to the nearest inch.

can of soup   _____ inches

pen   _____ inches

toothbrush   _____ inches

paper clip   _____ inches

small toy   _____ inches

cut out

8 7 6 5 4 3 2 1

Measurement

Directions: Use the ruler to measure the fish to the nearest inch.

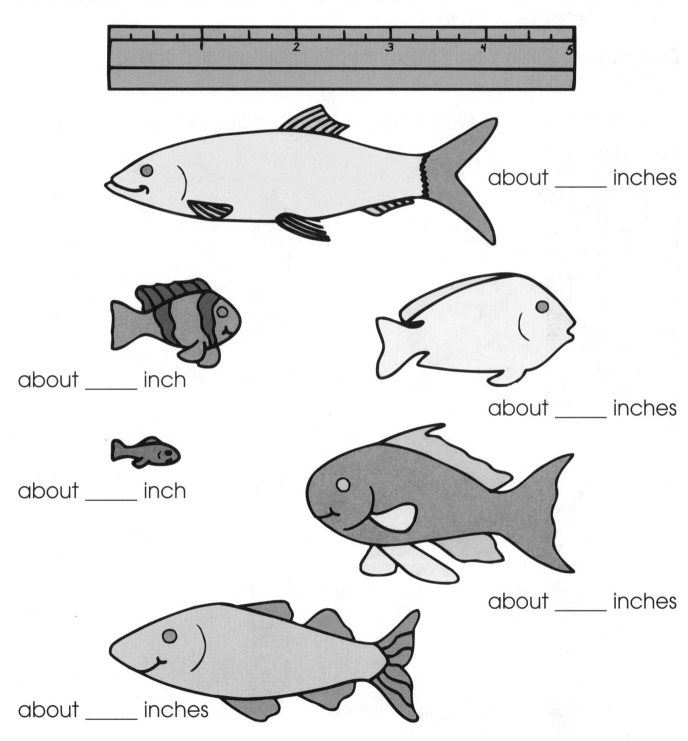

about _____ inches

about _____ inch

about _____ inches

about _____ inch

about _____ inches

about _____ inches

Name _____

Measurement: Centimeters

A **centimeter** is a unit of length in the metric system. There are 2.54 centimeters in an inch.

Directions: Use a centimeter ruler to measure the crayons to the nearest centimeter.

Example: The first crayon is about 7 centimeters long.

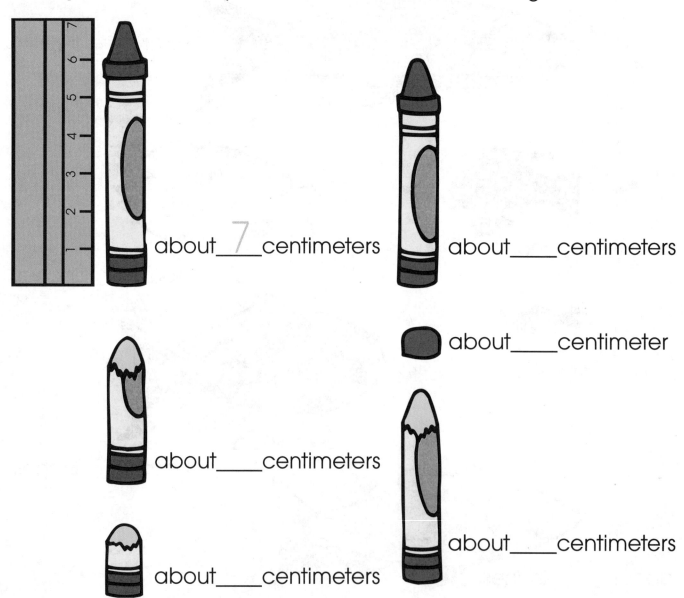

about __7__ centimeters

about ____ centimeters

about ____ centimeter

about ____ centimeters

about ____ centimeters

about ____ centimeters

Your Total Solution for Second Grade

Measurement: Centimeters

Directions: The giraffe is about 8 centimeters high. How many centimeters (cm) high are the trees? Write your answers in the blanks.

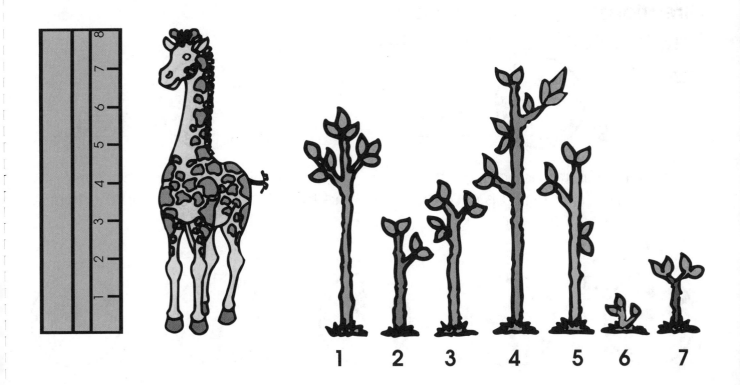

1   2   3   4   5   6   7

1)_____cm   2)_____cm   3)_____cm

4)_____cm   5)_____cm   6)_____cm   7)_____cm

Time: Hour, Half-Hour

An hour is sixty minutes. The short hand of a clock tells the hour. It is written **0:00**, such as **5:00**. A half-hour is thirty minutes. When the long hand of the clock is pointing to the six, the time is on the half-hour. It is written **:30**, such as **5:30**.

Directions: Study the examples.
Tell what time it is on each clock.

Examples:  **9:00**

 **4:30**

The minute hand is on the 12.
The hour hand is on the 9.
It is 9 o'clock.

The minute hand is on the 6.
The hour hand is *between* the 4 and 5.
It is 4:30.

_____ _____ _____ _____ _____

_____ _____ _____ _____ _____

Your Total Solution for Second Grade

Time: Hour, Half-Hour

Directions: Draw lines between the clocks that show the same time.

   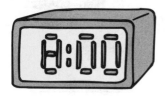

Name _____

Time: Counting by Fives

The minute hand of a clock takes 5 minutes to move from one number to the next. Start at the 12 and count by fives to tell how many minutes it is past the hour.

Directions: Study the examples. Tell what time is on each clock.

Examples:

 9:10

8:25

_____

_____

_____

_____

Your Total Solution for Second Grade

Time: Quarter-Hours

Time can also be shown as fractions. 30 minutes = $\frac{1}{2}$ hour.

Directions: Shade the fraction of each clock and tell how many minutes you have shaded.

Example: 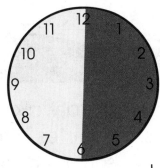 $\frac{1}{2}$ hour

30 minutes

 $\frac{1}{4}$ hour

___ minutes

 $\frac{2}{4}$ hour

___ minutes

 $\frac{3}{4}$ hour

___ minutes

 $\frac{1}{2}$ hour

___ minutes

Problem-Solving: Time

Directions: Solve each problem.

Tracy wakes up at 7:00. She has 30 minutes before her bus comes. What time does her bus come?

____ : _____

Vera walks her dog for 15 minutes after supper. She finishes supper at 6:30. When does she get home from walking her dog?

____ : _____

Chip practices the piano for 30 minutes when he gets home from school. He gets home at 3:30. When does he stop practicing?

____ : _____

Tanya starts mowing the grass at 4:30. She finishes at 5:00. For how many minutes does she mow the lawn?

_____ minutes

Dan does his homework for 45 minutes. He starts his work at 7:15. When does he stop working?

____ : _____

Your Total Solution for Second Grade

Money: Penny, Nickel

Penny **1¢**　　　Nickel **5¢**

Directions: Count the coins and write the amount.

Example:

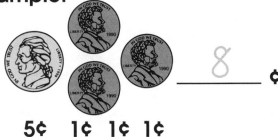

_____8_____ ¢

5¢　1¢　1¢　1¢

_____ ¢

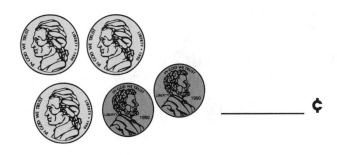

_____ ¢

_____ ¢

_____ ¢

Money: Penny, Nickel, Dime

Penny **1¢**   Nickel **5¢**   Dime **10¢**

Directions: Count the coins and write the amount.

_16_ ¢

_____ ¢

_____ ¢

_____ ¢

_____ ¢

Your Total Solution for Second Grade

Money: Penny, Nickel, Dime

Directions: Draw a line from the toy to the amount of money it costs.

Name _____

Money: Quarter

A quarter is worth 25¢.

Directions: Count the coins and write the amounts.

 _____ ¢

 _____ ¢

 _____ ¢

 _____ ¢

 _____ ¢

 _____ ¢

 _____ ¢

 _____ ¢

Your Total Solution for Second Grade

Money: Decimal

A decimal is a number with one or more places to the right of a decimal point, such as **6.5** or **2.25**. Money amounts are written with two places to the right of the decimal point.

25¢	10¢	5¢	1¢
$.25	$.10	$.05	$.01

Directions: Count the coins and circle the amount shown.

Example:

($.17)   23¢ $.07

$.50   51¢   61¢

$.28   36¢   42¢

37¢   43¢ $.47

Name _____

Money: Decimal

Directions: Draw a line from the coins to the correct amount in each column.

3¢ $.55

55¢ $.41

31¢ $.37

37¢ $.31

41¢ $.03

Your Total Solution for Second Grade

Money: Dollar

One dollar equals 100 cents. It is written **$1.00**.

Directions: Count the money and write the amounts.

 $___.____

 $___.____

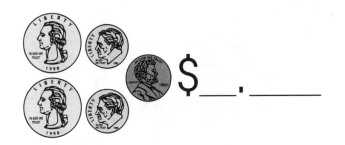 $___.____

 $___.____

 $___.____

 $___.____

 $___.____

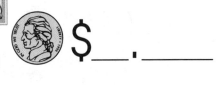

 $___.____

$___.____

Name _____

Adding Money

Directions: Write the amount of money using decimals. Then, add to find the total amount.

Example:

$$\begin{array}{r} \$1.00 \\ .05 \\ +\ .02 \\ \hline \$1.07 \end{array}$$

$ ___.___
$ ___.___
$ ___.___
+$ ___.___
_____
___.___

$ ___.___
$ ___.___
$ ___.___
+$ ___.___
_____
___.___

$ ___.___
$ ___.___
+$ ___.___
_____
___.___

$ ___.___
$ ___.___
$ ___.___
+$ ___.___
_____
___.___

Your Total Solution for Second Grade

Money: Practice

Directions: Draw a line from each food item to the correct amount of money.

$1.59

$.89

$1.27

$1.09

$.77

$1.95

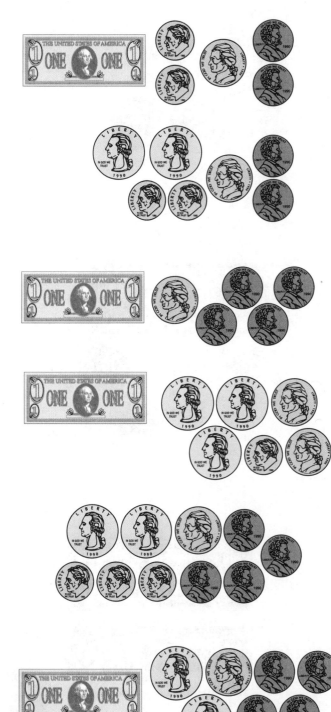

Name _____

Review

Directions: Add the money and write the total.

_____ ¢

_____ ¢

$ ____ . _____

_____ ¢

$ ____ . _____

Your Total Solution for Second Grade

Problem-Solving: Money

Directions: Read each problem. Use the pictures to help you solve the problems.

Ben bought a ball. He had 11¢ left.
How much money did he have at the start?   _____ ¢

Tara has 75¢. She buys a car.
How much money does she have left?   _____ ¢

Leah wants to buy a doll and a ball. She has 80¢.
How much more money does she need?   _____ ¢

Jacob has 95¢. He buys the car and the ball.
How much more money does he need to
buy a doll for his sister?   _____ ¢

Kim paid three quarters, one dime,
and three pennies for a hat.
How much did it cost?   _____ ¢

Name _____

Review

Two-Digit Addition and Subtraction

Directions: Add or subtract using regrouping, if needed.

66	38	87	52	40
− 37	+ 18	− 69	− 15	+ 17

84	65	99	61	56
+ 17	+ 14	− 48	− 36	+ 46

Place Value: Hundreds and Thousands

Directions: Draw a line to the correct number.

4 hundreds + 3 tens + 2 ones	7,201
6 hundreds + 7 tens + 6 ones	290
5 thousands + 3 hundreds + 7 tens + 2 ones	432
2 hundreds + 9 tens + 0 ones	676
7 thousands + 2 hundreds + 0 tens + 1 one	5,372

Three-Digit Addition and Subtraction

Directions: Add or subtract, remembering to regroup, if needed.

458	793	822	528	697	569
− 248	− 414	− 460	+ 319	+ 108	+ 288

Your Total Solution for Second Grade

Review

Multiplication

Directions: Solve the problems. Draw groups if necessary.

$$\begin{array}{r} 2 \\ \times\,8 \\ \hline 16 \end{array} \qquad \begin{array}{r} 6 \\ \times\,4 \\ \hline 24 \end{array} \qquad \begin{array}{r} 3 \\ \times\,2 \\ \hline 6 \end{array} \qquad \begin{array}{r} 8 \\ \times\,4 \\ \hline 32 \end{array} \qquad \begin{array}{r} 5 \\ \times\,3 \\ \hline 15 \end{array} \qquad \begin{array}{r} 2 \\ \times\,2 \\ \hline 4 \end{array}$$

Fractions

Directions: Circle the correct fraction of each shape's white part.

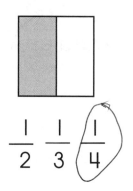

$$\frac{1}{2} \qquad \frac{1}{3} \qquad \boxed{\frac{1}{4}}$$

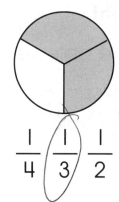

$$\frac{1}{4} \qquad \boxed{\frac{1}{3}} \qquad \frac{1}{2}$$

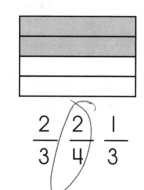

$$\frac{2}{3} \qquad \boxed{\frac{2}{4}} \qquad \frac{1}{3}$$

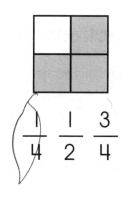

$$\boxed{\frac{1}{4}} \qquad \frac{1}{2} \qquad \frac{3}{4}$$

Graphs

Directions: Count the flowers. Color the pots to make a graph that shows the number of flowers.

1   2   3   4   5   6   7   8

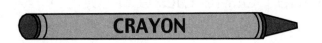
Review

Geometry

Directions: Match the shapes.

rectangle

square

circle

triangle

Measurement

Directions: Look at the ruler. Measure the objects to the nearest inch

$1 \quad 2 \quad 3 \quad 4 \quad 5$

_____ inches

_____ inches

CRAYON   _____ inches

Time

Directions: Tell what time is on each clock.

_____   _____   _____   _____

Answer Key

Beginning Consonants: b, c, d, f, g, h, j

Directions: Fill in the beginning consonant for each word.

Example: <u>c</u> at

<u>b</u> ox

<u>j</u> acket

<u>g</u> oat

<u>h</u> ouse

<u>d</u> og

<u>f</u> ire

6

Beginning Consonants: k, l, m, n, p, q, r

Directions: Write the letter that makes the beginning sound for each picture.

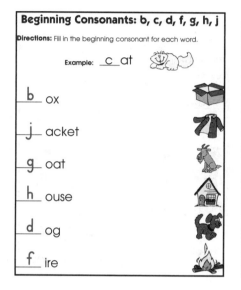

<u>m</u> <u>q</u> <u>r</u> <u>n</u>

<u>m</u> <u>l</u> <u>k</u> <u>r</u>

<u>q</u> <u>p</u> <u>n</u> <u>m</u>

<u>l</u> <u>k</u> <u>r</u> <u>p</u>

7

Beginning Consonants: s, t, v, w, x, y, z

Directions: Write the letter under each picture that makes the beginning sound.

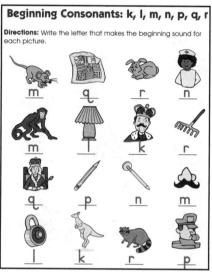

<u>s</u> <u>z</u>

<u>x</u>

<u>v</u>

<u>y</u>

<u>w</u> <u>t</u>

8

Ending Consonants: b, d, f, g

Directions: Fill in the ending consonant for each word.

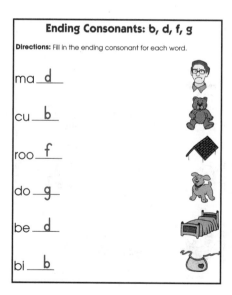

ma <u>d</u>

cu <u>b</u>

roo <u>f</u>

do <u>g</u>

be <u>d</u>

bi <u>b</u>

9

Ending Consonants: k, l, m, n, p, r

Directions: Fill in the ending consonant for each word.

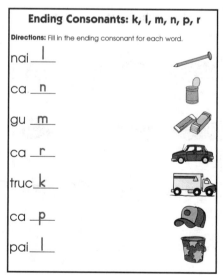

nai <u>l</u>

ca <u>n</u>

gu <u>m</u>

ca <u>r</u>

truc <u>k</u>

ca <u>p</u>

pai <u>l</u>

10

Ending Consonants: s, t, x

Directions: Fill in the ending consonant for each word.

ca <u>t</u>

bo <u>x</u>

bu <u>s</u>

fo <u>x</u>

boa <u>t</u>

ma <u>t</u>

11

Answer Key

Consonant Blends

Consonant blends are two or three consonant letters in a word whose sounds combine, or blend. **Examples:** br, fr, gr, pr, tr

Directions: Look at each picture. Say its name. Write the blend you hear at the beginning of each word.

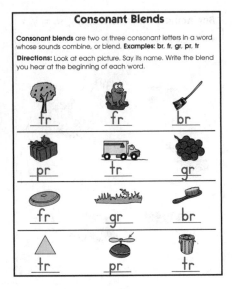

tr   fr   br

pr   tr   gr

fr   gr   br

tr   pr   tr

12

Consonant Blends: bl, sl, cr, cl

Directions: Look at the pictures and say their names. Write the letters for the beginning sound in each word.

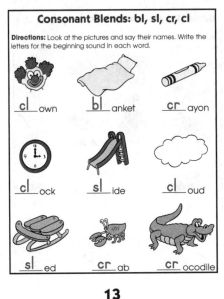

cl own   bl anket   cr ayon

cl ock   sl ide   cl oud

sl ed   cr ab   cr ocodile

13

Consonant Teams

Consonant teams are two or three consonant letters that have a single sound. **Examples:** sh and tch

Directions: Write each word from the word box next to its picture. Underline the consonant team in each word. Circle the consonant team in each word in the box.

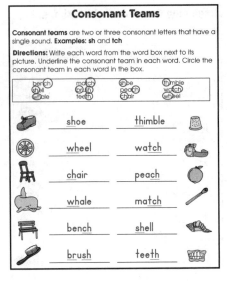

ben(ch)	mat(ch)	sh(oe)	(th)imble
(sh)ell	bru(sh)	pea(ch)	wa(tch)
(wh)ale	tee(th)	(ch)air	(wh)eel

shoe   thimble

wheel   watch

chair   peach

whale   match

bench   shell

brush   teeth

14

Consonant Teams

Directions: Read the words in the box. Write a word from the word box to finish each sentence. Circle the consonant team in each word. **Hint:** There are three letters in each team!

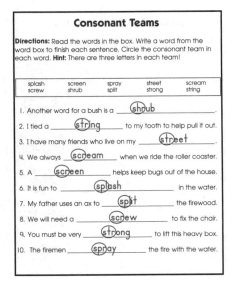

| splash | screen | spray | street | scream |
| screw | shrub | split | strong | string |

1. Another word for a bush is a (shr)ub
2. I tied a (str)ing to my tooth to help pull it out.
3. I have many friends who live on my (str)eet .
4. We always (scr)eam when we ride the roller coaster.
5. A (scr)een helps keep bugs out of the house.
6. It is fun to (spl)ash in the water.
7. My father uses an ax to (spl)it the firewood.
8. We will need a (scr)ew to fix the chair.
9. You must be very (str)ong to lift this heavy box.
10. The firemen (spr)ay the fire with the water.

15

Letter Teams: sh, ch, wh, th

Directions: Look at the first picture in each row. Circle the pictures that have the same sound.

16

Short Vowels

Vowels can make **short** or **long** sounds. The short **a** sounds like the **a** in **cat**. The short **e** is like the **e** in **leg**. The short **i** sounds like the **i** in **pig**. The short **o** sounds like the **o** in **box**. The short **u** sounds like the **u** in **cup**.

Directions: Look at each picture. Write the missing short vowel letter.

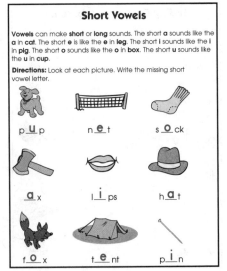

p u p   n e t   s o ck

a x   l i ps   h a t

f o x   t e nt   p i n

17

Your Total Solution for Second Grade

Answer Key

Short Vowels

Directions: Look at the pictures. Their names all have short vowel sounds. But the vowels are missing! Fill the missing vowels in each word.

p u pp e t   h a mmer   p o pcorn   e l e ph a nt

t e l e v i sion   b o ttle   sh o ve l   th i mble

c a ndle   bu tt o n   p e nny   l a dder

18

Short a Words

Directions: Use a word from the box to complete each sentence.

fat	path	lamp	can
van	stamp	Dan	math
sat	cat	fan	bat

Example:
1. The **lamp** had a pink shade.
2. The bike **path** led us to the park.
3. I like to add in **math** class.
4. The cat is very **fat**.
5. The **can** of beans was hard to open.
6. The envelope needed a **stamp**.
7. He swung the **bat** and hit the ball.
8. The **fan** blew air around.
9. My mom drives a blue **van**.
10. I **sat** in the backseat.

19

Short e Words

Directions: Say each word and listen for the short **e** sound. Then, write each word and underline the letter that makes the short **e** sound.

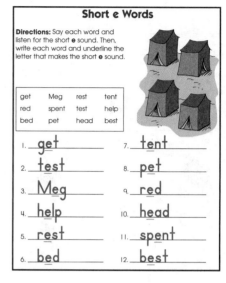

get	Meg	rest	tent
red	spent	test	help
bed	pet	head	best

1. g**e**t
2. t**e**st
3. M**e**g
4. h**e**lp
5. r**e**st
6. b**e**d
7. t**e**nt
8. p**e**t
9. r**e**d
10. h**e**ad
11. sp**e**nt
12. b**e**st

20

Short i Words

Directions: Complete the sentences by matching the words to the correct sentence.

1. I made a **wish** on a star. — fin
2. All we could see was the shark's **fin** above the water. — fish
3. I like to eat vegetables with **dip** — kick
4. We saw lots of **fish** in the water. — win
5. The soccer player will **kick** the ball and score a goal. — dish
6. If you feel **sick**, see a doctor. — dip
7. Did Bob **win** the race? — wish
8. The **dish** was full of candy. — sick

21

Short o Words

Directions: Use the short **o** words in the box to write rhyming words.

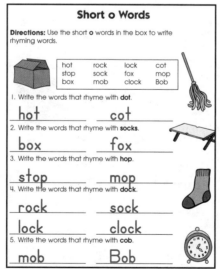

hot	rock	lock	cot
stop	sock	fox	mop
box	mob	clock	Bob

1. Write the words that rhyme with **dot**.
   hot   cot
2. Write the words that rhyme with **socks**.
   box   fox
3. Write the words that rhyme with **hop**.
   stop   mop
4. Write the words that rhyme with **dock**.
   rock   sock
   lock   clock
5. Write the words that rhyme with **cob**.
   mob   Bob

22

Short u Words

Directions: Say each word and listen for the short **u** sound. Then, write each word and underline the letter that makes the short **u** sound.

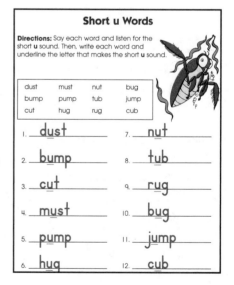

dust	must	nut	bug
bump	pump	tub	jump
cut	hug	rug	cub

1. d**u**st
2. b**u**mp
3. c**u**t
4. m**u**st
5. p**u**mp
6. h**u**g
7. n**u**t
8. t**u**b
9. r**u**g
10. b**u**g
11. j**u**mp
12. c**u**b

23

Answer Key

Long Vowels

Long vowel sounds have the same sound as their names. When a **Super Silent e** comes at the end of a word, you can't hear it, but it changes the vowel sound to a long vowel sound.

Example: rope, skate, bee, pie, cute

Directions: Say the name of the pictures. Listen for the long vowel sounds. Write the missing long vowel sound under each picture.

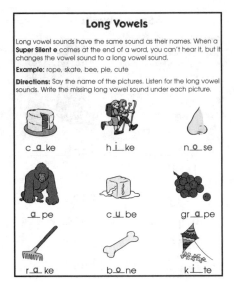

c _a_ ke   h _i_ ke   n _o_ se

_a_ pe   c _u_ be   gr _a_ pe

r _a_ ke   b _o_ ne   k _i_ te

24

Long a Words

Directions: Write the words in order so that each sentence tells a complete idea. Begin each sentence with a capital letter and end it with a period or a question mark.

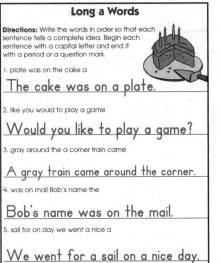

1. plate was on the cake a

The cake was on a plate.

2. like you would to play a game

Would you like to play a game?

3. gray around the a corner train came

A gray train came around the corner.

4. was on mail Bob's name the

Bob's name was on the mail.

5. sail for on day we went a nice a

We went for a sail on a nice day.

25

Long e Words

Long **e** is the vowel sound which says its own name. Long e can be spelled **ee** as in the word **teeth**, **ea** as in the word **meat**, or **e** as in the word **me**.

Directions: Say each word and listen for the long **e** sound. Then, write the words and underline the letters that make the long **e** sound.

street	neat	treat	feet
sleep	keep	deal	meal
mean	clean	beast	feast

1. street   7. treat
2. sleep   8. deal
3. mean   9. beast
4. neat   10. feet
5. keep   11. meal
6. clean   12. feast

26

Long i Words

Long **i** is the sound you hear in the word **fight**.

Directions: Use the long **i** words in the box to write rhyming words.

hide	ride	line	my
by	nine	high	light
sight	fly		

1. Write the words that rhyme with **sigh**.

high   my   by   fly

2. Write the words that rhyme with **side**.

hide   ride

3. Write the words that rhyme with **fine**.

line   nine

4. Write the words that rhyme with **fight**.

light   sight

27

Long o Words

Long **o** is the vowel sound which says its own name. Long **o** can be spelled **oa** as in the word **float** or **o** with a silent **e** at the end as in **cone**.

Directions: Say each word and listen for the long **o** sound. Then, write each word and underline the letters that make the long **o** sound.

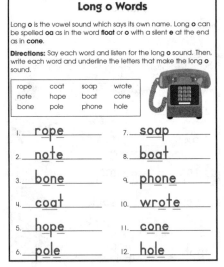

rope	coat	soap	wrote
note	hope	boat	cone
bone	pole	phone	hole

1. rope   7. soap
2. note   8. boat
3. bone   9. phone
4. coat   10. wrote
5. hope   11. cone
6. pole   12. hole

28

Long u Words

Directions: Write the words in the sentences below in the correct order. Begin each sentence with a capital letter and end it with a period or a question mark.

1. the pulled dentist tooth my loose

The dentist pulled my loose tooth.

2. ice cubes I choose in my drink to put

I choose to put ice cubes in my drink.

3. a Ruth fuse blew yesterday

Ruth blew a fuse yesterday.

4. loose the got in garden goose the

The goose got loose in the garden.

5. flew the goose winter for the south

The goose flew south for the winter.

6. is full there a moon tonight

Is there a full moon tonight?

29

Your Total Solution for Second Grade

Answer Key

Answer Key

Double Vowel Words

Usually when two vowels appear together, the first one says its name and the second one is silent.
Example: bean

Directions: Unscramble the double vowel words below. Write the correct word on the line.

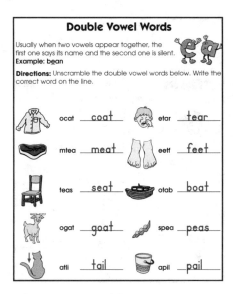

ocat	_coat_	etar	_tear_
mtea	_meat_	eetf	_feet_
teas	_seat_	otab	_boat_
ogat	_goat_	spea	_peas_
atli	_tail_	apil	_pail_

30

Vowel Teams

The vowel teams **ou** and **ow** can have the same sound. You can hear it in the words **clown** and **cloud**. The vowel teams **au** and **aw** have the same sound. You hear it in the words **because** and **law**.

Directions: Look at the pictures. Write the correct vowel team to complete the words. The first one is done for you. You may need to use a dictionary to help you with the correct spelling.

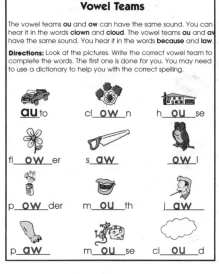

au_to   cl_ow_n   h_ou_se

fl_ow_er   s_aw_   _ow_l

p_ow_der   m_ou_th   j_aw_

p_aw_   m_ou_se   cl_ou_d

31

Vowel Teams

The vowel team **ea** can have a short **e** sound like in **head**, or a long **e** sound like in **bead**. An **ea** followed by an **r** makes a sound like the one in **ear** or like the one in **heard**.

Directions: Read the story. Listen for the sound ea makes in the bold words.

Have you ever **read** a book or **heard** a story about a **bear**? You might have **learned** that bears sleep through the winter. Some bears may sleep the whole **season**. Sometimes they look almost **dead**! But they are very much alive. As the cold winter passes and the spring **weather** comes **near**, they wake up. After such a nice rest, they must be **ready** to **eat** a really big **meal**!

words with long **ea**	words with short **ea**	**ea** followed by r
season	_read_	_heard_
eat	_dead_	_bear_
really	_weather_	_learned_
meal	_ready_	_near_

32

Vowel Teams

The vowel team **ie** makes the long **e** sound like in **believe**. The team **ei** also makes the long **e** sound like in **either**. But **ei** can also make a long **a** sound like in **eight**.

Directions: Circle the **ei** words with the long **a** sound.

(neighbor)   (veil)
receive   (reindeer)
(reign)   ceiling

The teams **eigh** and **ey** also make the long **a** sound.

Directions: Finish the sentences with words from the word box.

| chief | sleigh | obey | weigh | thief | field | ceiling |

1. Eight reindeer pull Santa's _sleigh_.
2. Rules are for us to _obey_.
3. The bird got out of its cage and flew up to the _ceiling_.
4. The leader of an Indian tribe is the _chief_.
5. How much do you _weigh_ ?
6. They caught the _thief_ who took my bike.
7. Corn grows in a _field_.

33

Vowel Teams: oi, oy, ou, ow

Directions: Look at the first picture in each row. Circle the pictures that have the same sound.

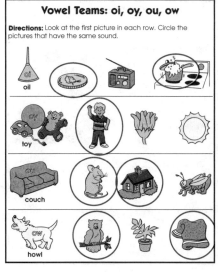

34

Vowel Teams: ai, ee

Directions: Write in the vowel team **ai** or **ee** to complete each word.

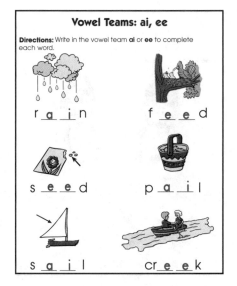

r_ai_n   f_ee_d

s_ee_d   p_ai_l

s_ai_l   cr_ee_k

35

Answer Key

Compound Words

Compound words are formed by putting together two smaller words.

Directions: Help the cook brew her stew. Mix words from the first column with words from the second column to make new words. Write your new words on the lines at the bottom.

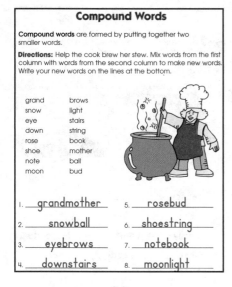

grand	brows
snow	light
eye	stairs
down	string
rose	book
shoe	mother
note	ball
moon	bud

1. grandmother
2. snowball
3. eyebrows
4. downstairs
5. rosebud
6. shoestring
7. notebook
8. moonlight

36

Compound Words

Directions: Read the sentences. Fill in the blank with a compound word from the box.

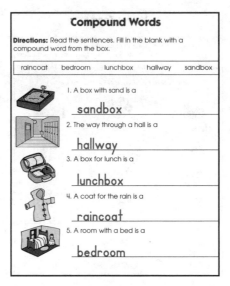

| raincoat | bedroom | lunchbox | hallway | sandbox |

1. A box with sand is a
   sandbox

2. The way through a hall is a
   hallway

3. A box for lunch is a
   lunchbox

4. A coat for the rain is a
   raincoat

5. A room with a bed is a
   bedroom

37

Compound Words

Directions: Draw a line under the compound word in each sentence. On the line, write the two words that make up the compound word.

1. A firetruck came to help put out the fire.
   fire   truck

2. I will be nine years old on my next birthday.
   birth   day

3. We built a treehouse at the back.
   tree   house

4. Dad put a scarecrow in his garden.
   scare   crow

5. It is fun to make footprints in the snow.
   foot   prints

6. I like to read the comics in the newspaper.
   news   paper

7. Cowboys ride horses and use lassos.
   cow   boys

38

Contractions

Contractions are a short way to write two words, such as **isn't**, **I've**, and **weren't**. Example: **it is = it's**

Directions: Draw a line from each word pair to its contraction.

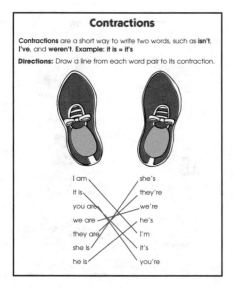

I am	she's
it is	they're
you are	we're
we are	he's
they are	I'm
she is	it's
he is	you're

39

Contractions

Directions: Circle the contraction that would replace the underlined words.

Example: were not = weren't

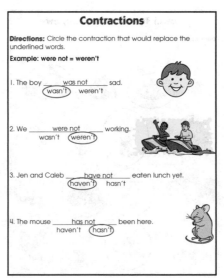

1. The boy was not sad.
   (wasn't)   weren't

2. We were not working.
   wasn't   (weren't)

3. Jen and Caleb have not eaten lunch yet.
   (haven't)   hasn't

4. The mouse has not been here.
   haven't   (hasn't)

40

Contractions

Directions: Match the words with their contractions.

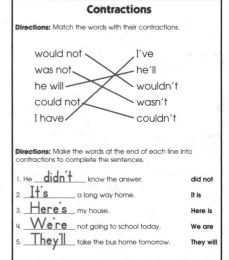

would not	I've
was not	he'll
he will	wouldn't
could not	wasn't
I have	couldn't

Directions: Make the words at the end of each line into contractions to complete the sentences.

1. He didn't know the answer.   **did not**
2. It's a long way home.   **It is**
3. Here's my house.   **Here is**
4. We're not going to school today.   **We are**
5. They'll take the bus home tomorrow.   **They will**

41

Your Total Solution for Second Grade

Answer Key

Syllables

Words are made up of parts called **syllables**. Each syllable has a vowel sound. One way to count syllables is to clap as you say the word.

Example:
cat	I clap	I syllable
table	2 claps	2 syllables
butterfly	3 claps	3 syllables

Directions: "Clap out" the words below. Write how many syllables each word has.

movie	2	dog	I
piano	3	basket	2
tree	I	swimmer	2
bicycle	3	rainbow	2
sun	I	paper	2
cabinet	3	picture	2
football	2	run	I
television	4	enter	2

42

Syllables

Dividing a word into syllables can help you read a new word. You also might divide syllables when you are writing if you run out of space on a line.

Many words contain two consonants that are next to each other. A word can usually be divided between the consonants.

Directions: Divide each word into two syllables. The first one is done for you.

kitten	kit	ten
lumber	lum	ber
batter	bat	ter
winter	win	ter
funny	fun	ny
harder	har	der
dirty	dir	ty
sister	sis	ter
little	lit	tle

43

Syllables

One way to help you read a word you don't know is to divide it into syllables. Every syllable has a vowel sound.

Directions: Say the words. Write the number of syllables. The first one is done for you.

straw • ber • ry

bird	I	rabbit	2
apple	2	elephant	3
balloon	2	family	3
basketball	3	fence	I
breakfast	2	ladder	2
block	I	open	2
candy	2	puddle	2
popcorn	2	Saturday	3
yellow	2	wind	I
understand	3	butterfly	3

44

Syllables

When a double consonant is used in the middle of a word, the word can usually be divided between the consonants.

Directions: Look at the words in the word box. Divide each word into two syllables. Leave space between each syllable. One is done for you.

butter	puppy	kitten	yellow
dinner	chatter	ladder	happy
pillow	letter	mitten	summer

but ter	chat ter	mit ten
din ner	let ter	yel low
pil low	kit ten	hap py
pup py	lad der	sum mer

Many words are divided between two consonants that are not alike.

Directions: Look at the words in the word box. Divide each word into two syllables. One is done for you.

window	doctor	number	carpet
mister	winter	pencil	candle
barber	sister	picture	under

win dow	win ter	pic ture
mis ter	sis ter	car pet
bar ber	num ber	can dle
doc tor	pen cil	un der

45

Suffixes

A **suffix** is a syllable that is added at the end of a word to change its meaning.

Directions: Add the suffixes to the root words to make new words. Use your new words to complete the sentences.

help + ful =	helpful
care + less =	careless
build + er =	builder
talk + ed =	talked
love + ly =	lovely
loud + er =	louder

1. My mother __talked__ to my teacher about my homework.
2. The radio was __louder__ than the television.
3. Sally is always __helpful__ to her mother.
4. A __builder__ put a new garage on our house.
5. The flowers are __lovely__.
6. It is __careless__ to cross the street without looking both ways.

46

Suffixes

Adding **ing** to a word means that it is happening now. Adding **ed** to a word means that it happened in the past.

Directions: Look at the words in the word box. Underline the root word in each one. Write a word to complete each sentence.

| snowing | wished | played | looking | crying |
| talking | walked | eating | going | doing |

1. We like to play. We __played__ yesterday.
2. Is that snow? Yes, it is __snowing__.
3. Do you want to go with me? No, I am __going__ with my friend.
4. The baby will cry if we leave. The baby is __crying__.
5. We will walk home from school. We __walked__ to school this morning.
6. Did you wish for a new bike? Yes, I __wished__ for one.
7. Who is going to do it while we are away? I am __doing__ it.
8. Did you talk to your friend? Yes, we are __talking__ now.
9. Will you look at my book? I am __looking__ at it now.
10. I like to eat pizza. We are __eating__ it today.

47

Answer Key

Suffixes

Directions: Write a word from the word box next to its root word.

coming	running	sitting
lived	rained	swimming
visited	carried	racing
hurried		

run	_running_	come	_coming_
live	_lived_	carry	_carried_
hurry	_hurried_	race	_racing_
swim	_swimming_	rain	_rained_
visit	_visited_	sit	_sitting_

Directions: Write a word from the word box to finish each sentence.

1. I _visited_ my grandmother during vacation.
2. Mary went _swimming_ at the lake with her cousin.
3. Jim _carried_ the heavy package for his mother.
4. It _rained_ and stormed all weekend.
5. Cars go very fast when they are _racing_.

48

Prefixes: The Three R's

Prefixes are syllables added to the beginning of words that change their meaning. The prefix **re** means "again."

Directions: Read the story. Then, follow the instructions.

Kim wants to find ways she can save Earth. She studies the "three R's"—reduce, reuse, and recycle. **Reduce** means "to make less." Both **reuse** and **recycle** mean "to use again." Add **re** to the beginning of each word below. Use the new words to complete the sentences.

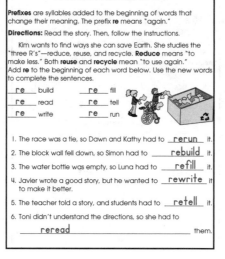

_re_ build	_re_ fill
_re_ read	_re_ tell
_re_ write	_re_ run

1. The race was a tie, so Dawn and Kathy had to _rerun_ it.
2. The block wall fell down, so Simon had to _rebuild_ it.
3. The water bottle was empty, so Luna had to _refill_ it.
4. Javier wrote a good story, but he wanted to _rewrite_ it to make it better.
5. The teacher told a story, and students had to _retell_ it.
6. Toni didn't understand the directions, so she had to _reread_ them.

49

Prefixes

Directions: Change the meaning of the sentences by adding the prefixes to the **bold** words.

The boy was **lucky** because he guessed the answer **correctly**.
The boy was (un) _unlucky_ because he guessed the answer (in) _incorrectly_.

When Mary **behaved**, she felt **happy**.
When Mary (mis) _misbehaved_, she felt (un) _unhappy_.

Mike wore his jacket **buttoned** because the dance was **formal**.
Mike wore his jacket (un) _unbuttoned_ because the dance was (in) _informal_.

Tim **understood** because he was **familiar** with the book.
Tim (mis) _misunderstood_ because he was (un) _unfamiliar_ with the book.

50

Synonyms

Words that mean the same or nearly the same are called **synonyms**.

Directions: Read the sentence that tells about the picture. Draw a circle around the word that means the same as the **bold** word.

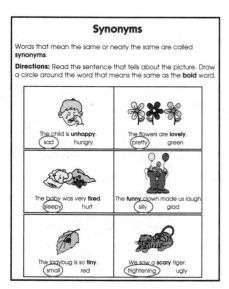

The child is **unhappy**. (sad) hungry
The flowers are **lovely**. (pretty) green
The baby was very **tired**. (sleepy) hurt
The **funny** clown made us laugh. (silly) glad
The ladybug is so **tiny**. (small) red
We saw a **scary** tiger. (frightening) ugly

51

Synonyms

Directions: Read the story. Then, fill in the blanks with the synonyms.

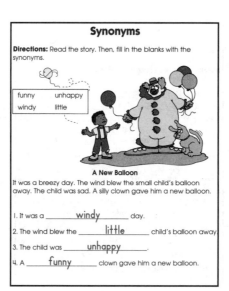

funny	unhappy
windy	little

A New Balloon

It was a breezy day. The wind blew the small child's balloon away. The child was sad. A silly clown gave him a new balloon.

1. It was a _windy_ day.
2. The wind blew the _little_ child's balloon away.
3. The child was _unhappy_.
4. A _funny_ clown gave him a new balloon.

52

Synonyms

Directions: Read each sentence. Fill in the blanks with the synonyms.

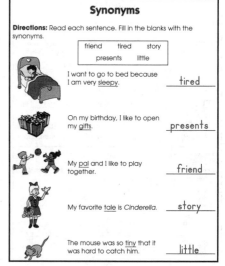

friend	tired	story
presents	little	

I want to go to bed because I am very <u>sleepy</u>. _tired_

On my birthday, I like to open my <u>gifts</u>. _presents_

My <u>pal</u> and I like to play together. _friend_

My favorite <u>tale</u> is Cinderella. _story_

The mouse was so <u>tiny</u> that it was hard to catch him. _little_

53

Your Total Solution for Second Grade

Answer Key

Antonyms

Antonyms are words that mean the opposite of another word.

Examples:
hot and **cold**
short and **tall**

Directions: Draw a line from each word on the left to its antonym on the right.

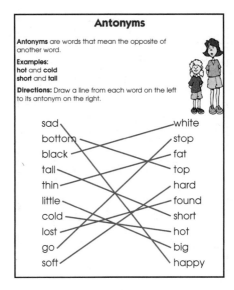

sad — white
bottom — stop
black — fat
tall — top
thin — hard
little — found
cold — short
lost — hot
go — big
soft — happy

54

Antonyms

Directions: Read the words next to the pictures. Draw a line to the antonyms.

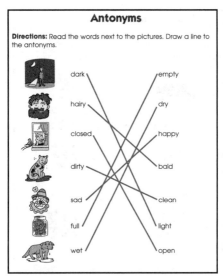

dark — empty
hairy — dry
closed — happy
dirty — bald
sad — clean
full — light
wet — open

55

Antonyms

Directions: Read the sentence. Write the word from the word box that means the opposite of the **bold** word.

| bottom | outside | black | summer | after |
| light | sister | clean | last | evening |

1. Lisa has a new baby **brother**. ___sister___
2. The class went **inside** for recess. ___outside___
3. There is a **white** car in the driveway. ___black___
4. We went to the park **before** dinner. ___after___
5. Joe's puppy is **dirty**. ___clean___
6. My name is at the **top** of the list. ___bottom___
7. I like to play outside in the **winter**. ___summer___
8. I like to take walks in the **morning**. ___evening___
9. The sky was **dark** after the storm. ___light___
10. Our team is in **first** place. ___last___

56

Homophones

Homophones are words that sound the same but are spelled differently and mean different things.

Directions: Write the homophone from the box next to each picture.

| so | see | blew | pear |

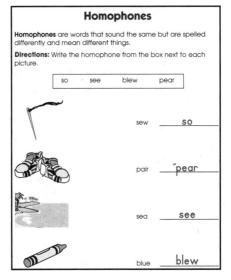

sew ___so___

pair ___pear___

sea ___see___

blue ___blew___

57

Homophones

Directions: Look at each picture. Circle the correct homophone.

(deer) dear
(two) to
by (bye)
ate (eight)
blue (blew)
hi (high)
(new) knew
(red) read

58

Homophones

Directions: Match each word with its homophone.

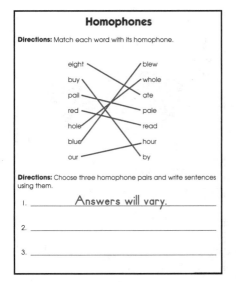

eight — blew
buy — whole
pail — ate
red — pale
hole — read
blue — hour
our — by

Directions: Choose three homophone pairs and write sentences using them.

1. ___Answers will vary.___

2. _____

3. _____

59

Answer Key

Nouns

A **noun** is the name of a person, place, or thing.

Directions: Read the story and circle all the nouns. Then, write the nouns next to the pictures below.

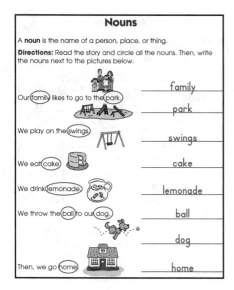

Our (family) likes to go to the (park.)

We play on the (swings)

We eat (cake)

We drink (lemonade)

We throw the (ball) to our (dog.)

Then, we go (home)

family
park
swings
cake
lemonade
ball
dog
home

60

Proper Nouns

Proper nouns are the names of specific people, places, and pets. Proper nouns begin with a capital letter.

Directions: Write the proper nouns on the lines below. Use capital letters at the beginning of each word.

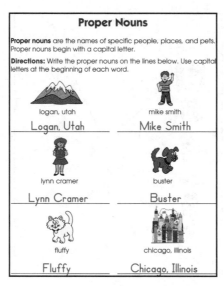

logan, utah
Logan, Utah

mike smith
Mike Smith

lynn cramer
Lynn Cramer

buster
Buster

fluffy
Fluffy

chicago, illinois
Chicago, Illinois

61

Proper Nouns

The days of the week and the months of the year are proper nouns.

Directions: Circle the words that are written correctly. Write the words that need capital letters on the lines below.

sunday	(July)	(Wednesday)	may	(Monday)
friday	tuesday	june	august	(April)
january	(February)	(March)	(Thursday)	
(September)	saturday	(October)	december	

Days of the Week		Months of the Year
1. Sunday	1.	January
2. Friday	2.	June
3. Tuesday	3.	May
4. Saturday	4.	August
	5.	December

62

Proper Nouns

The first word and all of the important words in a title begin with a capital letter.

Directions: Write the book titles on the lines below. Use capital letters.

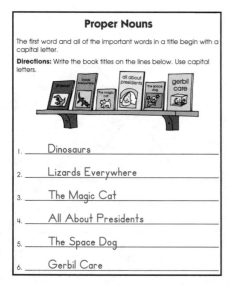

1. Dinosaurs
2. Lizards Everywhere
3. The Magic Cat
4. All About Presidents
5. The Space Dog
6. Gerbil Care

63

Plural Nouns

Plural nouns name more than one person, place, or thing.

Directions: Read the words in the box. Write the words in the correct column.

| hats | girl | cows | kittens | cake |
| spoons | glass | book | horse | trees |

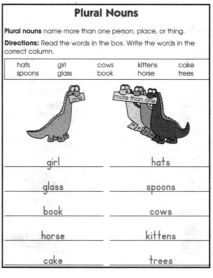

one	more than one
girl	hats
glass	spoons
book	cows
horse	kittens
cake	trees

64

Plurals

Plurals are words that mean more than one. You usually add an **s** or **es** to the word. In some words ending in **y**, the **y** changes to an **i** before adding **es**. For example, **baby** changes to **babies**.

Directions: Look at the following lists of plural words. Write the word that means one next to it. The first one has been done for you.

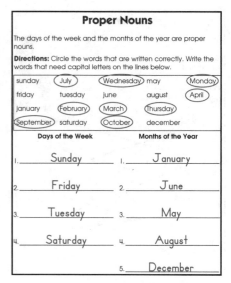

foxes	fox	balls	ball
bushes	bush	candles	candle
dresses	dress	wishes	wish
chairs	chair	boxes	box
shoes	shoe	ladies	lady
stories	story	bunnies	bunny
puppies	puppy	desks	desk
matches	match	dishes	dish
cars	car	pencils	pencil
glasses	glass	trucks	truck

65

Your Total Solution for Second Grade

Answer Key

More Than One

To show more than one of something, we add **s** to most words.
Example: one dog – **two dogs**   one book – **two books**
But some words are different. For words that end with **x**, use **es** to show two.
Example: one fox – **two foxes**   one box – **two boxes**
The spelling of some words changes a lot when there are two.
Example: one mouse – **two mice**
Some words stay the same, even when you mean two of something.
Example: one deer – **two deer**   one fish – **two fish**

Directions: Complete the sentences below with the correct word.

1. The _____ run fast.   **rabbits**

2. The _____ are eating   **deer**

3. Have you seen any _____ today?   **bears**

4. Where do the _____ live?   **foxes**

5. Did you ever have _____ for pets?   **mice**

66

Pronouns

Pronouns are words that can be used instead of nouns. **She**, **he**, **it**, and **they** are pronouns.

Directions: Read the sentence. Then, write the sentence again, using **she**, **he**, **it**, or **they** in the blank.

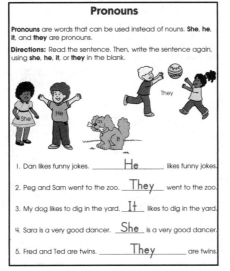

1. Dan likes funny jokes. _____ **He** _____ likes funny jokes.

2. Peg and Sam went to the zoo. **They** _____ went to the zoo.

3. My dog likes to dig in the yard. **It** _____ likes to dig in the yard.

4. Sara is a very good dancer. **She** _____ is a very good dancer.

5. Fred and Ted are twins. **They** _____ are twins.

67

Verbs

A **verb** is the action word in a sentence. Verbs tell what something does or that something exists.

Example: Run, **sleep**, and **jump** are verbs.

Directions: Circle the verbs in the sentences below.

1. We (play) baseball everyday.

2. Susan (pitches) the ball very well.

3. Mike (swings) the bat harder than anyone.

4. Chris (slides) into home base.

5. Laura (hit) a home run.

68

Verbs

We use verbs to tell when something happens. Sometimes we add an **ed** to verbs that tell us if something has already happened.

Example: Today, we will **play**. Yesterday, we **played**.

Directions: Write the correct verb in the blank.

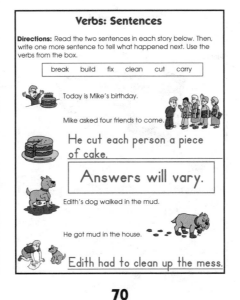

1. Today, I will **wash** my dog, Fritz.
   (wash)   washed

2. Last week, Fritz **cried** when we said, "Bath time, Fritz."
   cry   (cried)

3. My sister likes to **help** wash Fritz.
   (help)   helped

4. One time she **cleaned** Fritz by herself.
   clean   (cleaned)

5. Fritz will **look** a lot better after his bath.
   (look)   looked

69

Verbs: Sentences

Directions: Read the two sentences in each story below. Then, write one more sentence to tell what happened next. Use the verbs from the box.

break	build	fix	clean	cut	carry

Today is Mike's birthday.

Mike asked four friends to come.

He cut each person a piece of cake. _____

Answers will vary.

Edith's dog walked in the mud.

He got mud in the house.

Edith had to clean up the mess.

70

Is, Are, and Am

Is, **are**, and **am** are special action words that tell us something is happening now.
Use **am** with **I**. **Example: I am**.
Use **is** to tell about one person or thing. **Example: He is**.
Use **are** to tell about more than one. **Example: We are**.
Use **are** with you. **Example: You are**.

Directions: Write **is**, **are**, or **am** in the sentences below.

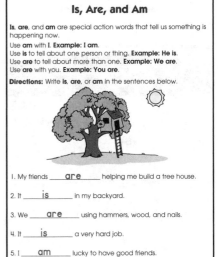

1. My friends **are** helping me build a tree house.

2. It **is** in my backyard.

3. We **are** using hammers, wood, and nails.

4. It **is** a very hard job.

5. I **am** lucky to have good friends.

71

Answer Key

Was and Were

Was and were tell us about something that already happened. Use was to tell about one person or thing. Example: I was, he was. Use were to tell about more than one person or thing or when using the word you. Example: We were, you were.

Directions: Write was or were in each sentence.

1. Lily _____was_____ eight years old on her birthday.

2. Tim and Steve _____were_____ happy to be at the party.

3. Megan _____was_____ too shy to sing "Happy Birthday."

4. Ben _____was_____ sorry he dropped his cake.

5. All of the children _____were_____ happy to be invited.

72

Go, Going, and Went

We use go or going to tell about now or later. Sometimes we use going with the words am or are. We use went to tell about something that already happened.

Directions: Write go, going, or went in the sentences below.

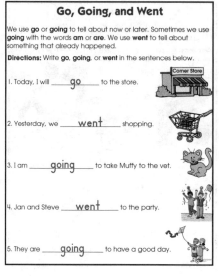

1. Today, I will _____go_____ to the store.

2. Yesterday, we _____went_____ shopping.

3. I am _____going_____ to take Muffy to the vet.

4. Jan and Steve _____went_____ to the party.

5. They are _____going_____ to have a good day.

73

Have, Has, and Had

We use have and has to tell about now. We use had to tell about something that already happened.

Directions: Write has, have, or had in the sentences below.

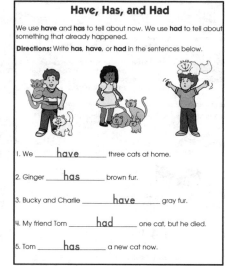

1. We _____have_____ three cats at home.

2. Ginger _____has_____ brown fur.

3. Bucky and Charlie _____have_____ gray fur.

4. My friend Tom _____had_____ one cat, but he died.

5. Tom _____has_____ a new cat now.

74

See, Saw, and Sees

We use see or sees to tell about now. We use saw to tell about something that already happened.

Directions: Write see, sees, or saw in the sentences below.

1. Last night, we _____saw_____ the stars.

2. John can _____see_____ the stars from his window.

3. He _____sees_____ them every night.

4. Last week, he _____saw_____ the Big Dipper.

5. Can you _____see_____ it in the night sky, too?

6. If you _____saw_____ it, you would remember it!

7. John _____sees_____ it often now.

8. How often do you _____see_____ it?

75

Eat, Eats, and Ate

We use eat or eats to tell about now. We use ate to tell about what already happened.

Directions: Write eat, eats, or ate in the sentences below.

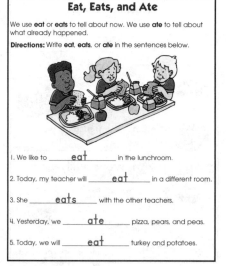

1. We like to _____eat_____ in the lunchroom.

2. Today, my teacher will _____eat_____ in a different room.

3. She _____eats_____ with the other teachers.

4. Yesterday, we _____ate_____ pizza, pears, and peas.

5. Today, we will _____eat_____ turkey and potatoes.

76

Leave, Leaves, and Left

We use leave and leaves to tell about now. We use left to tell about what already happened.

Directions: Write leave, leaves, or left in the sentences below.

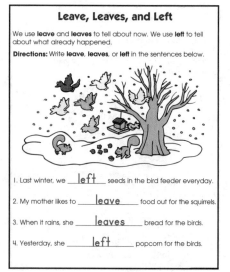

1. Last winter, we _____left_____ seeds in the bird feeder everyday.

2. My mother likes to _____leave_____ food out for the squirrels.

3. When it rains, she _____leaves_____ bread for the birds.

4. Yesterday, she _____left_____ popcorn for the birds.

77

Your Total Solution for Second Grade

Answer Key

Adjectives

Adjectives are words that tell more about a person, place, or thing.

Examples: cold, fuzzy, dark

Directions: Circle the adjectives in the sentences.

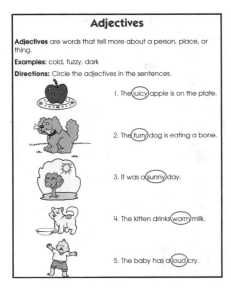

1. The (juicy) apple is on the plate.

2. The (furry) dog is eating a bone.

3. It was a (sunny) day.

4. The kitten drinks (warm) milk.

5. The baby has a (loud) cry.

78

Adjectives

Directions: Choose an adjective from the box to fill in the blanks.

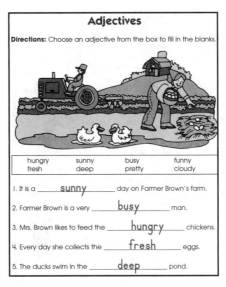

| hungry | sunny | busy | funny |
| fresh | deep | pretty | cloudy |

1. It is a _____ **sunny** _____ day on Farmer Brown's farm.

2. Farmer Brown is a very _____ **busy** _____ man.

3. Mrs. Brown likes to feed the _____ **hungry** _____ chickens.

4. Every day she collects the _____ **fresh** _____ eggs.

5. The ducks swim in the _____ **deep** _____ pond.

79

Adjectives

Directions: Think of your own adjectives. Write a story about Fluffy the cat.

Answers will vary.

1. Fluffy is a _____ cat.

2. The color of his fur is _____.

3. He likes to chew on my _____ shoes.

4. He likes to eat _____ cat food.

5. I like Fluffy because he is so _____.

80

Subjects

The **subject** of a sentence is the person, place, or thing the sentence is about.

Directions: Underline the subject in each sentence.

Example: Mom read a book.
(Think: Who is the sentence about? Mom)

1. The <u>bird</u> flew away.

2. The <u>kite</u> was high in the air.

3. The <u>children</u> played a game.

4. The <u>books</u> fell down.

5. The <u>monkey</u> climbed a tree.

81

Compound Subjects

Two similar sentences can be joined into one sentence if the predicate is the same. A **compound subject** is made up of two subjects joined together by the word **and**.

Example: Jamie can sing.
Sandy can sing.
<u>Jamie</u> **and** <u>Sandy</u> can sing.

Directions: Combine the sentences. Write the new sentence on the line.

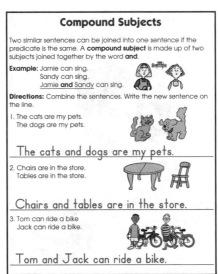

1. The cats are my pets.
The dogs are my pets.

The cats and dogs are my pets.

2. Chairs are in the store.
Tables are in the store.

Chairs and tables are in the store.

3. Tom can ride a bike.
Jack can ride a bike.

Tom and Jack can ride a bike.

82

Predicates

The **predicate** is the part of the sentence that tells about the action.

Directions: Circle the predicate in each sentence.

Example: The boys ran on the playground.
(Think: The boys did what? (Ran))

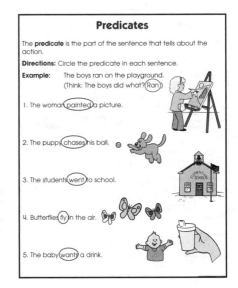

1. The woman (painted) a picture.

2. The puppy (chases) his ball.

3. The students (went) to school.

4. Butterflies (fly) in the air.

5. The baby (wants) a drink.

83

Answer Key

Subjects and Predicates

The **subject** part of the sentence is the person, place, or thing the sentence is about. The **predicate** is the part of the sentence that tells what the subject does.

Directions: Draw a line between the subject and the predicate. Underline the noun in the subject and circle the verb.

Example: The furry cat (ate) food.

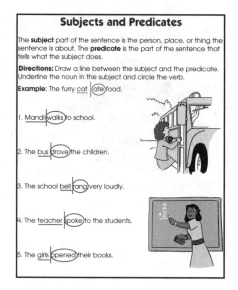

1. Mandi (walks) to school.

2. The bus (drove) the children.

3. The school bell (rang) very loudly.

4. The teacher (spoke) to the students.

5. The girls (opened) their books.

84

Parts of a Sentence

Directions: Draw a circle around the noun, the naming part of the sentence. Draw a line under the verb, the action part of the sentence.

Example: (John) drinks juice every morning. 🎵

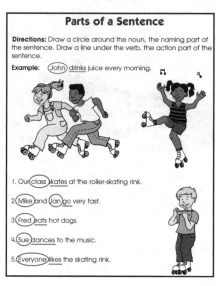

1. Our (class) skates at the roller-skating rink.

2. (Mike) and (Jan) go very fast.

3. (Fred) eats hot dogs.

4. (Sue) dances to the music.

5. (Everyone) likes the skating rink.

85

Parts of a Sentence

Directions: Look at the pictures. Draw a line from the naming part of the sentence to the action part to complete the sentence.

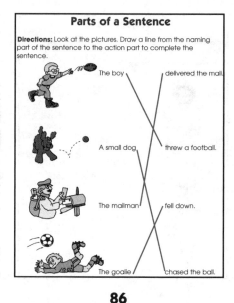

The boy — threw a football.

A small dog — chased the ball.

The mailman — delivered the mail.

The goalie — fell down.

86

Sentences and Non-Sentences

A **sentence** tells a complete idea. It has a noun and a verb. It begins with a capital letter and has punctuation at the end.

Directions: Circle the group of words if it is a sentence.

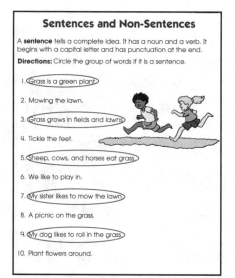

1. (Grass is a green plant.)

2. Mowing the lawn.

3. (Grass grows in fields and lawns.)

4. Tickle the feet.

5. (Sheep, cows, and horses eat grass.)

6. We like to play in.

7. (My sister likes to mow the lawn.)

8. A picnic on the grass.

9. (My dog likes to roll in the grass.)

10. Plant flowers around.

87

Sentences and Non-Sentences

Directions: Circle the group of words if it tells a complete idea.

1. (A secret is something you know.)

2. (My mom's birthday gift is a secret.)

3. No one else.

4. If you promise not to.

5. (I'll tell you a secret.)

6. Something nobody knows.

88

Statements

Statements are sentences that tell us something. They begin with a capital letter and end with a period.

Directions: Write the sentences on the lines below. Begin each sentence with a capital letter and end it with a period.

1. we like to ride our bikes

We like to ride our bikes.

2. we go down the hill very fast

We go down the hill very fast.

3. we keep our bikes shiny and clean

We keep our bikes shiny and clean.

4. we know how to change the tires

We know how to change the tires.

89

Your Total Solution for Second Grade

Answer Key

Surprising Sentences

Surprising sentences tell a strong feeling and end with an exclamation point. A surprising sentence may be only one or two words showing fear, surprise, or pain. **Example: Oh, no!**

Directions: Put a period at the end of the sentences that tell something. Put an exclamation point at the end of the sentences that tell a strong feeling. Put a question mark at the end of the sentences that ask a question.

1. The cheetah can run very fast.
2. Wow!
3. Look at that cheetah go!
4. Can you run fast?
5. Oh, my!
6. You're faster than I am.
7. Let's run together.
8. We can run as fast as a cheetah.
9. What fun!
10. Do you think cheetahs get tired?

90

Commands

Commands tell someone to do something. **Example: "Be careful."** It can also be written as "Be careful!" if it tells a strong feeling.

Directions: Put a period at the end of the command sentences. Use an exclamation point if the sentence tells a strong feeling. Write your own commands on the lines below.

1. Clean your room.
2. Now!
3. Be careful with your goldfish.
4. Watch out!
5. Be a little more careful.

Answers will vary.

91

Questions

Questions are sentences that ask something. They begin with a capital letter and end with a question mark.

Directions: Write the questions on the lines below. Begin each sentence with a capital letter and end it with a question mark.

1. will you be my friend
   Will you be my friend?
2. what is your name
   What is your name?
3. are you eight years old
   Are you eight years old?
4. do you like rainbows
   Do you like rainbows?

92

Ownership

We add **'s** to nouns (people, places, or things) to tell who or what owns something.

Directions: Read the sentences. Fill in the blanks to show ownership.

Example: The doll belongs to **Sara**.
It is **Sara's** doll.

1. Sparky has a red collar.
   Sparky's collar is red.
2. Jimmy has a blue coat.
   Jimmy's coat is blue.
3. The tail of the cat is short.
   The cat's tail is short.
4. The name of my mother is Karen.
   My mother's name is Karen.

93

Ownership

Directions: Read the sentences. Choose the correct word and write it in the sentences below.

1. The boy's lunchbox is broken.   boys (boy's)
2. The gerbils played in the cage.   gerbil's (gerbils)
3. Ann's hair is brown.   Anns (Ann's)
4. The horses ran in the field.   horse's (horses)
5. My sister's coat is torn.   (sister's) sisters
6. The cat's fur is brown.   cats (cat's)
7. Three birds flew past our window.   (birds) bird's
8. The dog's paws are muddy.   dogs (dog's)
9. The giraffe's neck is long.   giraffes (giraffe's)
10. The lions are big and powerful.   lion's (lions)

94

Following Directions

Directions: Read the story. Answer the questions. Try the recipe.

Cows Give Us Milk

Cows live on a farm. The farmer milks the cow to get milk. Many things are made from milk. We make ice cream, sour cream, cottage cheese, and butter from milk. Butter is fun to make! You can learn to make your own butter. First, you need cream. Put the cream in a jar and shake it. Then, you need to pour off the liquid. Next, you put the butter in a bowl. Add a little salt and stir! Finally, spread it on crackers and eat!

1. What animal gives us milk? cow
2. What four things are made from milk?
   ice cream   sour cream   cottage cheese   butter
3. What did the story teach you to make? butter
4. Put the steps in order. Write 1, 2, 3, and 4 by the sentences.
   4 Spread the butter on crackers and eat!
   2 Shake cream in a jar.
   1 Start with cream.
   3 Add salt to the butter.

95

Answer Key

Following Directions: Ladybugs

Directions: Read about how to treat ladybugs. Then, follow the instructions.

Ladybugs are shy. If you see a ladybug, sit very still. Hold out your arm. Maybe the ladybug will fly to you. If it does, talk softly. Do not touch it. It will fly away when it is ready.

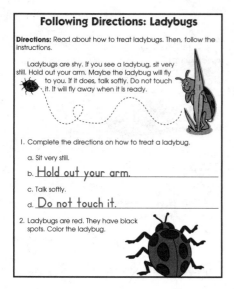

1. Complete the directions on how to treat a ladybug.

   a. Sit very still.

   b. _Hold out your arm._

   c. Talk softly.

   d. _Do not touch it._

2. Ladybugs are red. They have black spots. Color the ladybug.

96

Sequencing: Packing Bags

Directions: Read about packing bags. Then, number the objects in the order they should be packed.

Cans are heavy. Put them in first. Then, put in boxes. Now, put in the apple. Put the bread in last.

3 — apple
1 — soup cans
2 — cereal
4 — bread

97

Sequencing: Story Events

Spencer likes to make new friends. Today, he made friends with the dog in the picture.

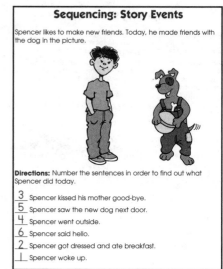

Directions: Number the sentences in order to find out what Spencer did today.

3 — Spencer kissed his mother good-bye.

5 — Spencer saw the new dog next door.

4 — Spencer went outside.

6 — Spencer said hello.

2 — Spencer got dressed and ate breakfast.

1 — Spencer woke up.

98

Sequencing: Yo-Yo Trick

Directions: Read about the yo-yo trick.

Wind up the yo-yo string. Hold the yo-yo in your hand. Now, hold your palm up. Throw the yo-yo downward on the string. Hold your palm down. Now, swing the yo-yo forward. Make it "walk." This yo-yo trick is called "Walk the Dog."

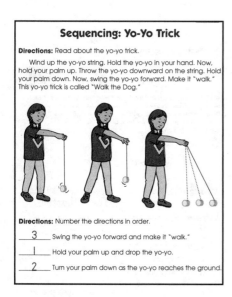

Directions: Number the directions in order.

3 — Swing the yo-yo forward and make it "walk."

1 — Hold your palm up and drop the yo-yo.

2 — Turn your palm down as the yo-yo reaches the ground.

99

Sequencing: Story Events

Mari was sick yesterday.

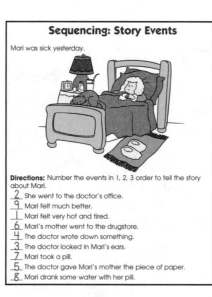

Directions: Number the events in 1, 2, 3 order to tell the story about Mari.

2 — She went to the doctor's office.

9 — Mari felt much better.

1 — Mari felt very hot and tired.

6 — Mari's mother went to the drugstore.

4 — The doctor wrote down something.

3 — The doctor looked in Mari's ears.

7 — Mari took a pill.

5 — The doctor gave Mari's mother the piece of paper.

8 — Mari drank some water with her pill.

100

Sequencing: Making Clay

Directions: Read about making clay. Then, follow the instructions.

It is fun to work with clay. Here is what you need to make it:

1 cup salt
2 cups flour
$\frac{3}{4}$ cup water

Mix the salt and flour. Then, add the water. DO NOT eat the clay. It tastes bad. Use your hands to mix and mix. Now, roll it out. What can you make with your clay?

1. Circle the main idea:

   Do not eat clay.

   (Mix salt, flour, and water to make clay.)

2. Write the steps for making clay.

   a. _Mix the salt and flour._

   b. _Add the water._

   c. Mix the clay.

   d. _Roll it out._

3. Write why you should not eat clay. _It tastes bad._

101

Your Total Solution for Second Grade

Answer Key

Sequencing: A Visit to the Zoo

Directions: Read the story. Then, follow the instructions.

One Saturday morning in May, Gloria and Anna went to the zoo. First, they bought tickets to get into the zoo. Second, they visited the Gorilla Garden and had fun watching the gorillas stare at them. Then, they went to Tiger Town and watched the tigers as they slept in the sunshine. Fourth, they went to Hippo Haven and laughed at the hippos cooling off in their pool. Next, they visited Snake Station and learned about poisonous and nonpoisonous snakes. It was noon, and they were hungry, so they ate lunch at the Parrot Patio.

Write **first, second, third, fourth, fifth,** and **sixth** to put the events in order.

Fourth — They went to Hippo Haven.

First — Gloria and Anna bought zoo tickets.

Third — They watched the tigers sleep.

Sixth — They ate lunch at Parrot Patio.

Second — The gorillas stared at them.

Fifth — They learned about poisonous and nonpoisonous snakes.

102

Same and Different: Stuffed Animals

Kate and Oralia like to collect and trade stuffed animals.

Directions: Draw two stuffed animals that are alike and two that are different.

Alike

Different

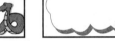 Answers will vary.

103

Same and Different: Cats and Tigers

Directions: Read about cats and tigers. Then, complete the Venn diagram, telling how they are the same and different.

Tigers are a kind of cat. Pet cats and tigers both have fur. Pet cats are small and tame. Tigers are large and wild.

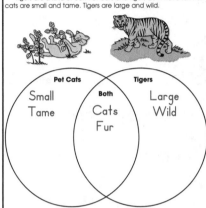

Pet Cats — Small Tame

Both — Cats Fur

Tigers — Large Wild

104

Same and Different: Birds

Directions: Read about parrots and bluebirds. Then, complete the Venn diagram, telling how they are the same and different.

Bluebirds and parrots are both birds. Bluebirds and parrots can fly. They both have beaks. Parrots can live inside a cage. Bluebirds must live outdoors.

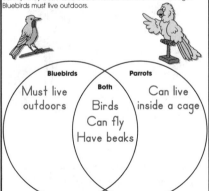

Bluebirds — Must live outdoors

Both — Birds Can fly Have beaks

Parrots — Can live inside a cage

105

Similes

A **simile** is a figure of speech that compares two different things. The words **like** or **as** are used in similes.

Directions: Draw a line to the picture that goes with each set of words.

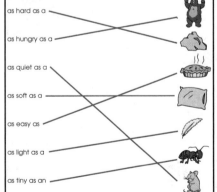

as hard as a

as hungry as a

as quiet as a

as soft as a

as easy as

as light as a

as tiny as an

106

Classifying: Outdoor/Indoor Games

Classifying is putting things that are alike into groups.

Directions: Read about games. Draw an **X** on the games you can play indoors. Circle the objects used for outdoor games.

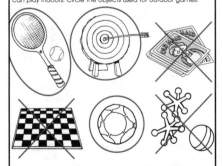

Some games are outdoor games. Some games are indoor games. Outdoor games are active. Indoor games are quiet. Which do you like best? Answers will vary.

107

Answer Key

Classifying

Directions: Write each word from the word box on the correct line.

| baby | donkey | whale | family | fox |
| uncle | goose | grandfather | kangaroo | policeman |

people   animals

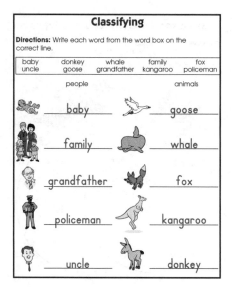

baby   goose

family   whale

grandfather   fox

policeman   kangaroo

uncle   donkey

108

Classifying: Animals

Directions: Use a red crayon to circle the names of three animals that would make good pets. Use a blue crayon to circle the names of three wild animals. Use an orange crayon to circle the two animals that live on a farm.

BEAR CAT LION SHEEP BIRD DOG COW TIGER

A	M	E	O	W	W	N	L	I	O	N
B	M	D	O	G	G	X	I	I	S	O
A	B	E	A	R	R	V	L	M	H	R
R	M	R	M	O	O	U	S	E	E	K
K	C	A	B	B	I	R	D	S	E	M
I	O	T	T	I	G	E	R	M	P	Q
B	W	N	O	W	W	R	Q	N	E	N
D	N	C	P	H	H	I	D	U	D	N
F	K	C	A	T	T	R	O	A	R	M

109

Opposite Words

Directions: Opposites are words that are different in every way. Use the opposite word from the box to complete these sentences.

| hard | hot | bottom | quickly | happy |
| sad | slowly | cold | soft | top |

Example:

My new coat is blue on **top** and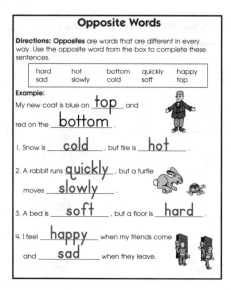

red on the **bottom**

1. Snow is **cold**, but fire is **hot**

2. A rabbit runs **quickly**, but a turtle

moves **slowly**

3. A bed is **soft**, but a floor is **hard**

4. I feel **happy** when my friends come

and **sad** when they leave.

110

Opposite Words

Directions: Draw a line from each sentence to its picture. Then, complete each sentence with the word under the picture.

Example:

She bought a **new** bat.

1. I like my **soft** pillow.

2. Birthdays make me **happy**

3. Put that book on **top**

4. Jenny runs **quickly**

5. A rock makes a **hard** seat.

6. I feel **sad** when it rains.

7. He eats **slowly**

hard

new

top

sad

slowly

quickly

happy

soft

111

Comprehension: Types of Tops

The **main idea** is the most important point or idea in a story.

Directions: Read about tops. Then, answer the questions.

Tops come in all sizes. Some tops are made of wood. Some tops are made of tin. All tops do the same thing. They spin! Do you have a top?

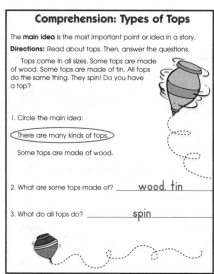

1. Circle the main idea:

There are many kinds of tops.

Some tops are made of wood.

2. What are some tops made of? **wood, tin**

3. What do all tops do? **spin**

112

Comprehension: Sea Horses

Directions: Read about sea horses. Then, answer the questions.

Sea horses are fish, not horses. A sea horse's head looks like a horse's head. It has a tail like a monkey's tail. A sea horse looks very strange!

1. (Circle the correct answer.)
   A sea horse is a kind of

   horse.

   monkey.

   fish.

2. What does a sea horse's head look like?

   a horse's head

3. What makes a sea horse look strange?

   a. **It's head looks like a horse's head.**

   b. **It has a tail like a monkey's tail.**

113

Answer Key

Comprehension: Dog Fights

Directions: Read about how to stop a dog fight. Then, answer the questions.

Sometimes dogs fight. They bark loudly. They may bite. Do not try to pull apart fighting dogs. Turn on a hose and spray them with water. This will stop the fight.

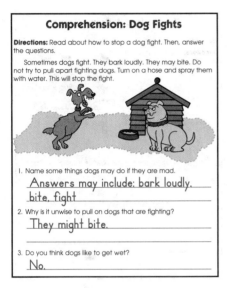

1. Name some things dogs may do if they are mad.
   Answers may include: bark loudly, bite, fight

2. Why is it unwise to pull on dogs that are fighting?
   They might bite.

3. Do you think dogs like to get wet?
   No.

114

Comprehension: How to Meet a Dog

Directions: Read about how to meet a dog. Then, follow the instructions.

Do not try to pet a dog right away. First, let the dog sniff your hand. Do not move quickly. Do not talk loudly. Just let the dog sniff.

1. Predict what the dog will let you do if it likes you.
   Pet it.

2. What should you let the dog do? Sniff your hand.

3. Name three things you should not do when you meet a dog.
   1) try to pet it
   2) move quickly
   3) talk loudly

115

Comprehension: Pretty Parrots

Directions: Read about parrots. Then, follow the instructions.

Big parrots are pretty. Their feet have four toes each. Two toes are in front. Two toes are in back. Parrots use their feet to climb. They use them to hold food.

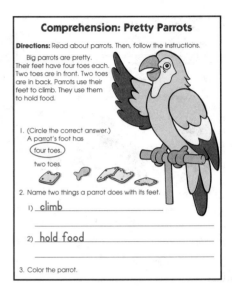

1. (Circle the correct answer.)
   A parrot's foot has
   (four toes.)
   two toes.

2. Name two things a parrot does with its feet.
   1) climb
   2) hold food

3. Color the parrot.

116

Comprehension: The Puppet Play

Directions: Read the play out loud with a friend. Then, answer the questions.

Pip: Hey, Pep. What kind of turkey eats very fast?

Pep: Uh, I don't know.

Pip: A gobbler!

Pep: I have a good joke for you, Pip. What kind of burger does a polar bear eat?

Pip: Uh, a cold burger?

Pep: No, an iceberg-er!

Pip: Hey, that was a great joke!

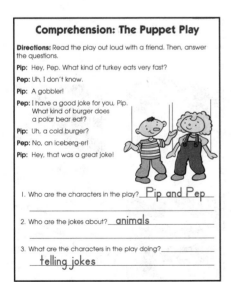

1. Who are the characters in the play? Pip and Pep

2. Who are the jokes about? animals

3. What are the characters in the play doing? telling jokes

117

Comprehension: Snakes!

Directions: Read about snakes. Then, answer the questions.

There are many facts about snakes that might surprise someone. A snake's skin is dry. Most snakes are shy. They will hide from people. Snakes eat mice and rats. They do not chew them up. Snakes' jaws drop open to swallow their food whole.

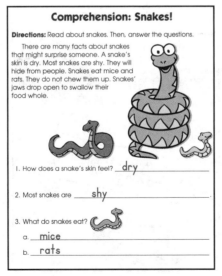

1. How does a snake's skin feel? dry

2. Most snakes are shy

3. What do snakes eat?
   a. mice
   b. rats

118

Comprehension: Sean's Basketball Game

Directions: Read about Sean's basketball game. Then, answer the questions.

Sean really likes to play basketball. One sunny day, he decided to ask his friends to play basketball at the park, but there were six people—Sean, Aki, Lance, Kate, Zac, and Oralia. A basketball team only allows five to play at a time. So, Sean decided to be the coach. Sean and his friends had fun.

1. How many kids wanted to play basketball? six

2. Write their names in ABC order:
   Aki   Kate   Lance
   Oralia   Sean   Zac

3. How many players can play on a basketball team at a time? five

4. Where did they play basketball? at the park

5. Who decided to be the coach? Sean

119

Answer Key

Comprehension: Amazing Ants

Directions: Read about ants. Then, answer the questions.

Ants are insects. Ants live in many parts of the world and make their homes in soil, sand, wood, and leaves. Most ants live for about 6 to 10 weeks. But the queen ant, who lays the eggs, can live for up to 15 years!

The largest ant is the bulldog ant. This ant can grow to be 5 inches long, and it eats meat! The bulldog ant can be found in Australia.

1. Where do ants make their homes? __in soil, sand, wood, and leaves__

2. How long can a queen ant live? __up to 15 years__

3. What is the largest ant? __bulldog ant__

4. What does it eat? __meat__

120

Comprehension: Fish

Directions: Read about fish. Then, follow the instructions.

Some fish live in warm water. Some live in cold water. Some fish live in lakes. Some fish live in oceans. There are 20,000 kinds of fish!

1. Name two types of water in which fish live.
   a. __warm water__
   b. __cold water__

   Some fish live in lakes and some live in __oceans__.

2. Name another place fish live __Answers may include: fish tank, ponds__

3. There are __20,000__ kinds of fish.

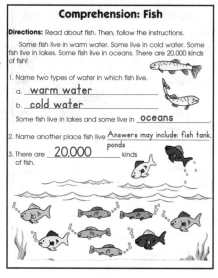

121

Predicting: A Rainy Game

Predicting is telling what is likely to happen based on the facts.

Directions: Read the story. Then, check each sentence below that tells how the story could end.

One cloudy day, Juan and his baseball team, the Bears, played the Crocodiles. It was the last half of the fifth inning, and it started to rain. The coaches and umpires had to decide what to do.

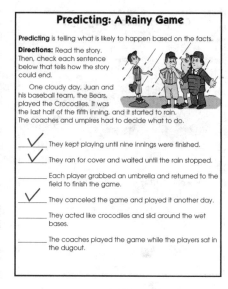

✓ They kept playing until nine innings were finished.

✓ They ran for cover and waited until the rain stopped.

_____ Each player grabbed an umbrella and returned to the field to finish the game.

✓ They canceled the game and played it another day.

_____ They acted like crocodiles and slid around the wet bases.

_____ The coaches played the game while the players sat in the dugout.

122

Predicting: Dog Derby

Directions: Read the story. Then, answer the questions.

Marcy had a great idea for a game to play with her dogs, Marvin and Mugsy. The game was called "Dog Derby." Marcy would stand at one end of the driveway and hold on to the dogs by their collars. Her friend Mitch would stand at the other end of the driveway. When he said, "Go!" Marcy would let go of the dogs and they would race to Mitch. The first one there would get a dog biscuit. If there was a tie, both dogs would get a biscuit.

1. Who do you think will win the race?

Why? _____

Answers will vary.

2. What _____ en when they race again?

_____

123

Predicting: Dog-Gone!

Directions: Read the story. Then, follow the instructions.

Scotty and Simone were washing their dog, Willis. His fur was wet. Their hands were wet. Willis did not like to be wet. Scotty dropped the soap. Simone picked it up and let go of Willis. Uh-oh!

1. Write what happened next.

_____

2. Draw wh_____

Answers and drawings will vary.

124

Predicting: At the Zoo

Directions: Read the story. Complete the story in the last box.

1. "Look at that elephant! He sure is big!"

2. "I'm hungry." "I bet that elephant is, too."

3. "Stop, Amy! Look at that sign!"

4. __Answers will vary.__

Drawings will vary.

125

Your Total Solution for Second Grade

Answer Key

Ordinal Numbers

Ordinal numbers indicate order in a series, such as **first**, **second**, or **third**.

Directions: Follow the instructions to color the train cars. The first car is the engine.

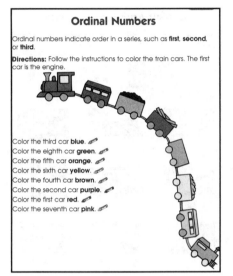

Color the third car **blue**.
Color the eighth car **green**.
Color the fifth car **orange**.
Color the sixth car **yellow**.
Color the fourth car **brown**.
Color the second car **purple**.
Color the first car **red**.
Color the seventh car **pink**.

151

Ordinal Numbers

Directions: Follow the instructions.

Draw glasses on the second one.
Put a hat on the fourth one.
Color blonde hair on the third one.
Draw a tie on the first one.
Draw ears on the fifth one.
Draw black hair on the seventh one.
Put a bow on the head of the sixth one.

152

Addition

Addition is "putting together" or adding two or more numbers to find the sum.

Directions: Add.

Example:

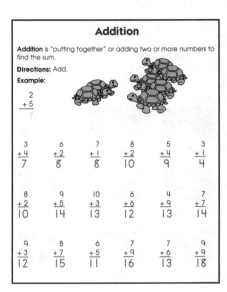

$$\begin{array}{r} 2 \\ +5 \\ \hline 7 \end{array}$$

$$\begin{array}{r} 3 \\ +4 \\ \hline 7 \end{array} \quad \begin{array}{r} 6 \\ +2 \\ \hline 8 \end{array} \quad \begin{array}{r} 7 \\ +1 \\ \hline 8 \end{array} \quad \begin{array}{r} 8 \\ +2 \\ \hline 10 \end{array} \quad \begin{array}{r} 5 \\ +4 \\ \hline 9 \end{array} \quad \begin{array}{r} 3 \\ +1 \\ \hline 4 \end{array}$$

$$\begin{array}{r} 8 \\ +2 \\ \hline 10 \end{array} \quad \begin{array}{r} 9 \\ +5 \\ \hline 14 \end{array} \quad \begin{array}{r} 10 \\ +3 \\ \hline 13 \end{array} \quad \begin{array}{r} 6 \\ +6 \\ \hline 12 \end{array} \quad \begin{array}{r} 4 \\ +9 \\ \hline 13 \end{array} \quad \begin{array}{r} 7 \\ +7 \\ \hline 14 \end{array}$$

$$\begin{array}{r} 9 \\ +3 \\ \hline 12 \end{array} \quad \begin{array}{r} 8 \\ +7 \\ \hline 15 \end{array} \quad \begin{array}{r} 6 \\ +5 \\ \hline 11 \end{array} \quad \begin{array}{r} 7 \\ +9 \\ \hline 16 \end{array} \quad \begin{array}{r} 7 \\ +6 \\ \hline 13 \end{array} \quad \begin{array}{r} 9 \\ +9 \\ \hline 18 \end{array}$$

153

Addition: Commutative Property

The commutative property of addition states that even if the order of the numbers is changed in an addition sentence, the sum will stay the same.

Example: $2 + 3 = 5$
$3 + 2 = 5$

Directions: Look at the addition sentences below. Complete the addition sentences by writing the missing numerals.

$5 + 4 = 9$ $3 + 1 = 4$ $2 + 6 = 8$
$4 + \underline{5} = 9$ $1 + \underline{3} = 4$ $6 + \underline{2} = 8$

$6 + 1 = 7$ $4 + 3 = 7$ $1 + 9 = 10$
$1 + \underline{6} = 7$ $3 + \underline{4} = 7$ $9 + \underline{1} = 10$

Now try these:

$6 + 3 = 9$ $10 + 2 = 12$ $8 + 3 = 11$
$\underline{3} + 6 = 9$ $\underline{2} + \underline{10} = 12$ $\underline{3} + \underline{8} = 11$

Look at these sums. Can you think of two number sentences that would show the commutative property of addition?

___ + ___ = 7   ___ + ___ = 11   ___ + ___ = 9

___ + ___ = 7   ___ + ___ = 11   ___ + ___ = 9

Answers will vary.

154

Adding Three or More Numbers

Directions: Add all the numbers to find the sum. Draw pictures to help or break up the problem into two smaller problems.

Example:

$$\begin{array}{r} 1 \\ 2 \\ +3 \\ \hline 6 \end{array} \quad\quad \begin{array}{r} 2 \\ 2 \\ +4 \\ \hline \end{array} \begin{array}{l} \Big\} \; 7 \\ \Big\} \; +6 \\ \hline 13 \end{array}$$

$$\begin{array}{r} 3 \\ 6 \\ +2 \\ \hline 11 \end{array} \Big\}9 \quad \begin{array}{r} 8 \\ 5 \\ +4 \\ \hline 17 \end{array}\Big\}9 \quad \begin{array}{r} 3 \\ 1 \\ +5 \\ \hline 9 \end{array}\Big\}4 \quad \begin{array}{r} 8 \\ 2 \\ +9 \\ \hline 19 \end{array}\Big\}10$$

$$\begin{array}{r} 2 \\ 8 \\ 4 \\ +3 \\ \hline 17 \end{array}\begin{array}{l}\Big\}10 \\ \Big\}\;7\end{array} \quad \begin{array}{r} 3 \\ 6 \\ 5 \\ +2 \\ \hline 16 \end{array}\begin{array}{l}\Big\}9 \\ \Big\}7\end{array} \quad \begin{array}{r} 4 \\ 1 \\ 2 \\ +5 \\ \hline 12 \end{array}\begin{array}{l}\Big\}5 \\ \Big\}7\end{array} \quad \begin{array}{r} 6 \\ 7 \\ 3 \\ +1 \\ \hline 17 \end{array}\begin{array}{l}\Big\}13 \\ \Big\}4\end{array}$$

155

Two-Digit Addition

Directions: Study the example. Follow the steps to add.

Example:

$$\begin{array}{r} 33 \\ +41 \\ \hline \end{array}$$

Step 1: Add the ones.

tens	ones
3	3
+4	1
	4

Step 2: Add the tens.

tens	ones
3	3
+4	1
7	4

tens	ones
4	2
+2	4
6	6

tens	ones
5	0
+4	7
9	7

$$\begin{array}{r} 24 \\ +62 \\ \hline 86 \end{array} \; \begin{array}{r} 15 \\ +23 \\ \hline 38 \end{array} \; \begin{array}{r} 38 \\ +61 \\ \hline 99 \end{array} \; \begin{array}{r} 11 \\ +26 \\ \hline 37 \end{array} \; \begin{array}{r} 37 \\ +42 \\ \hline 79 \end{array} \; \begin{array}{r} 72 \\ +11 \\ \hline 83 \end{array} \; \begin{array}{r} 33 \\ +51 \\ \hline 84 \end{array} \; \begin{array}{r} 10 \\ +30 \\ \hline 40 \end{array}$$

$$\begin{array}{r} 25 \\ +42 \\ \hline 67 \end{array} \; \begin{array}{r} 62 \\ +14 \\ \hline 76 \end{array} \; \begin{array}{r} 32 \\ +44 \\ \hline 76 \end{array} \; \begin{array}{r} 25 \\ +13 \\ \hline 38 \end{array} \; \begin{array}{r} 82 \\ +6 \\ \hline 88 \end{array} \; \begin{array}{r} 91 \\ +5 \\ \hline 96 \end{array} \; \begin{array}{r} 16 \\ +71 \\ \hline 87 \end{array} \; \begin{array}{r} 55 \\ +3 \\ \hline 58 \end{array}$$

156

Answer Key

Two-Digit Addition

Directions: Add the total points scored in each game. Remember to add **ones** first and **tens** second.

Example:

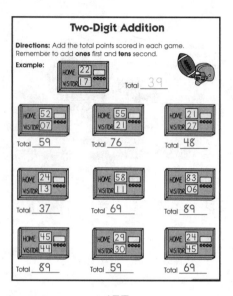

Total 39

Total 59   Total 76   Total 48

Total 37   Total 69   Total 89

Total 89   Total 59   Total 69

157

Two-Digit Addition: Regrouping

Addition is "putting together" or adding two or more numbers to fir the sum. Regrouping is using **ten ones** to form **one ten**, **ten tens** to form **one 100**, **fifteen ones** to form **one ten** and **five ones**, and so or

Directions: Study the examples. Follow the steps to add.

Example: 14 + 8

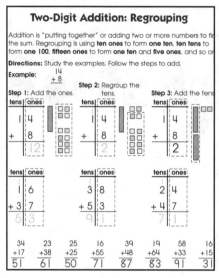

	tens	ones
	1	6
+	3	7
	5	3

	tens	ones
	3	8
+	5	3
	9	1

	tens	ones
	2	4
+	4	7
	7	1

34	23	25	16	39	19	58	16
+17	+38	+25	+55	+48	+64	+33	+15
51	61	50	71	87	83	91	31

158

Two-Digit Addition: Regrouping

Directions: Add the total points scored in the game. Remember to add the ones, regroup, and then add the tens.

Example:

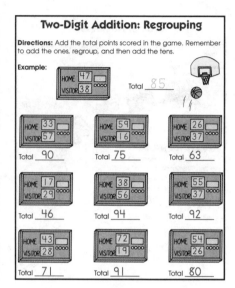

Total 85

Total 90   Total 75   Total 63

Total 46   Total 94   Total 92

Total 71   Total 91   Total 80

159

Three-Digit Addition: Regrouping

Directions: Study the examples. Follow the steps to add.

Example:

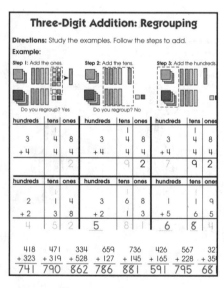

hundreds	tens	ones
3	4	8
+4	4	4
		2

hundreds	tens	ones
3	4	8
+4	4	4
	9	2

hundreds	tens	ones
3	4	8
+4	4	4
7	9	2

hundreds	tens	ones
2	1	4
+2	3	8
4	5	2

hundreds	tens	ones
3	6	8
+2	1	3
5	8	1

hundreds	tens	ones
1	1	9
+5	6	5
6	8	4

418	471	334	659	736	426	567	32
+323	+319	+528	+127	+145	+165	+228	+35
741	790	862	786	881	591	795	68

160

Three-Digit Addition: Regrouping

Directions: Study the example. Follow the steps to add. Regroup when needed.

Step 1: Add the ones.
Step 2: Add the tens.
Step 3: Add the hundreds.

hundreds	tens	ones
3	4	8
+4	5	4
8	0	2

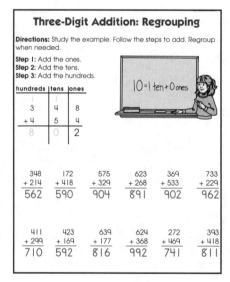

10 = 1 ten + 0 ones

348	172	575	623	369	733
+214	+418	+329	+268	+533	+229
562	590	904	891	902	962

411	423	639	624	272	393
+299	+169	+177	+368	+469	+418
710	592	816	992	741	811

161

Subtraction

Subtraction is "taking away" or subtracting one number from another to find the difference.

Directions: Subtract.

Example:

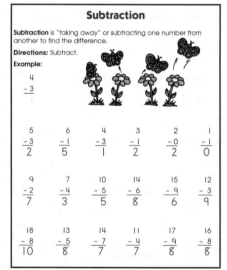

4
− 3
1

5	6	4	3	2	1
−3	−1	−3	−1	−0	−1
2	5	1	2	2	0

9	7	10	14	15	12
−2	−4	−5	−6	−9	−3
7	3	5	8	6	9

18	13	14	11	17	16
−8	−5	−7	−4	−9	−8
10	8	7	7	8	8

162

Your Total Solution for Second Grade

Answer Key

Two-Digit Subtraction

Directions: Study the example. Follow the steps to subtract.

Example:
$$\begin{array}{r} 28 \\ -14 \end{array}$$

Step 1: Subtract the ones.

Step 2: Subtract the tens.

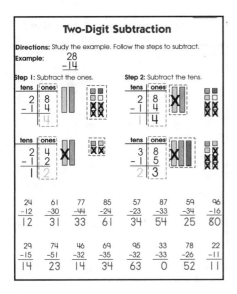

24	61	77	85	57	87	59	96
−12	−30	−44	−24	−23	−33	−34	−16
12	31	33	61	34	54	25	80

29	74	46	69	95	33	78	22
−15	−51	−32	−35	−32	−33	−26	−11
14	23	14	34	63	0	52	11

163

Two-Digit Subtraction: Regrouping

Subtraction is "taking away" or subtracting one number from another to find the difference. Regrouping is using **one ten** to form **ten ones**, **one 100** to form **ten tens**, and so on.

Directions: Study the examples. Follow the steps to subtract.

Example:
$$\begin{array}{r} 37 \\ -19 \end{array}$$

Step 1: Regroup.

Step 2: Subtract the ones.

Step 3: Subtract the tens.

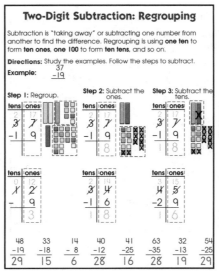

48	33	14	40	41	63	32	54
−19	−18	− 8	−12	−25	−35	−13	−25
29	15	6	28	16	28	19	29

164

Two-Digit Subtraction: Regrouping

Directions: Study the steps for subtracting. Solve the problems using the steps.

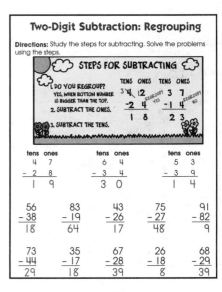

tens ones	tens ones	tens ones
4 7	6 4	5 3
− 2 8	− 3 4	− 3 9
1 9	3 0	1 4

56	83	43	75	91
− 38	− 19	− 26	− 27	− 82
18	64	17	48	9

73	35	67	26	68
− 44	− 17	− 28	− 18	− 29
29	18	39	8	39

165

Three-Digit Subtraction: Regrouping

Directions: Study the example. Follow the steps to subtract.

Step 1: Regroup ones.
Step 2: Subtract ones.
Step 3: Subtract tens.
Step 4: Subtract hundreds.

Example:

hundreds	tens	ones
4	6	2
− 2	5	3
2	0	9

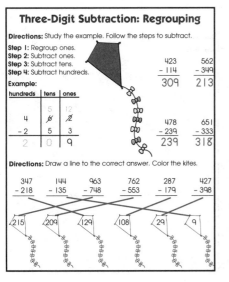

423	562
− 114	− 349
309	213

478	651
− 239	− 333
239	318

Directions: Draw a line to the correct answer. Color the kites.

347	144	963	762	287	427
− 218	− 135	− 748	− 553	− 179	− 398

215	209	129	108	29	9

166

Three-Digit Subtraction: Regrouping

Directions: Subtract. Circle the 7s that appear in the **tens place**.

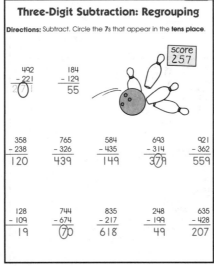

score
257

492	184
− 221	− 129
271	55

358	765	584	693	921
− 238	− 326	− 435	− 314	− 362
120	439	149	379	559

128	744	835	248	635
− 109	− 674	− 217	− 199	− 428
19	70	618	49	207

167

Addition and Subtraction

Directions: Add or subtract. Circle the answers that are less than 10.

Examples:

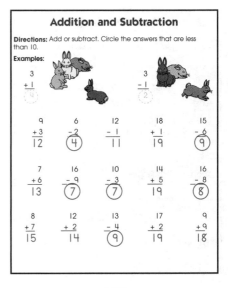

3	3
+1	−1
4	2

9	6	12	18	15
+3	−2	−1	+1	−6
12	4	11	19	9

7	16	10	14	16
+6	−9	−3	+5	−8
13	7	7	19	8

8	12	13	17	9
+7	+2	−4	+2	+9
15	14	9	19	18

168

Answer Key

Review

Directions: Add or subtract. Use regrouping when needed. Always do ones first and tens last.

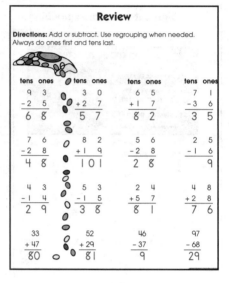

tens ones	tens ones	tens ones	tens ones
9 3 − 2 5 **6 8**	3 0 + 2 7 **5 7**	6 5 + 1 7 **8 2**	7 1 − 3 6 **3 5**
7 6 − 2 8 **4 8**	8 2 + 1 9 **1 0 1**	5 6 − 2 8 **2 8**	2 5 − 1 6 **9**
4 3 − 1 4 **2 9**	5 3 − 1 5 **3 8**	2 4 + 5 7 **8 1**	4 8 + 2 8 **7 6**
33 + 47 **80**	52 + 29 **81**	46 − 37 **9**	97 − 68 **29**

169

Two-Digit Addition and Subtraction

Directions: Add or subtract using regrouping.

Example:

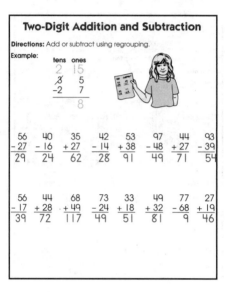

tens ones
2 15   3̶ 5   − 2 7   **8**

56 − 27 **29**	40 − 16 **24**	35 + 27 **62**	42 − 14 **28**	53 + 38 **91**	97 − 48 **49**	44 + 27 **71**	93 − 39 **54**
56 − 17 **39**	44 + 28 **72**	68 + 49 **117**	73 − 24 **49**	33 + 18 **51**	49 + 32 **81**	77 − 68 **9**	27 + 19 **46**

170

Two-Digit Addition and Subtraction

Directions: Add or subtract using regrouping.

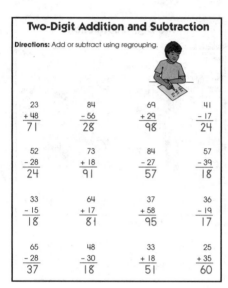

23 + 48 **71**	84 − 56 **28**	69 + 29 **98**	41 − 17 **24**
52 − 28 **24**	73 + 18 **91**	84 − 27 **57**	57 − 39 **18**
33 − 15 **18**	64 + 17 **81**	37 + 58 **95**	36 − 19 **17**
65 − 28 **37**	48 − 30 **18**	33 + 18 **51**	25 + 35 **60**

171

Problem-Solving

Directions: Tell whether you should add or subtract. "In all" is a clue to add. "Left" is a clue to subtract. Draw pictures to help you.

Example:

Jane's dog has 5 bones. He ate 3 bones. How many bones are left?

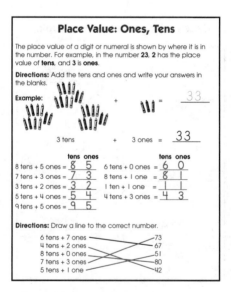

subtract

5
 − 3
 2 bones

Lucky the cat had 5 mice. She got 4 more for her birthday. How many mice did she have in all?

add

5
 + 4
 9 mice

Sam bought 6 fish. She gave 2 fish to a friend. How many fish does she have left?

subtract

6
 − 2
 4 fish

172

Place Value: Ones, Tens

The place value of a digit or numeral is shown by where it is in the number. For example, in the number **23**, **2** has the place value of **tens**, and **3** is **ones**.

Directions: Add the tens and ones and write your answers in the blanks.

Example:

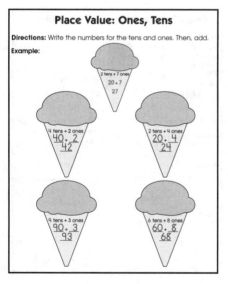

3 tens + 3 ones = **33**

	tens ones		tens ones
8 tens + 5 ones =	**8 5**	6 tens + 0 ones =	**6 0**
7 tens + 3 ones =	**7 3**	8 tens + 1 one =	**8 1**
3 tens + 2 ones =	**3 2**	1 ten + 1 one =	**1 1**
5 tens + 4 ones =	**5 4**	4 tens + 3 ones =	**4 3**
9 tens + 5 ones =	**9 5**		

Directions: Draw a line to the correct number.

6 tens + 7 ones — 73
4 tens + 2 ones — 67
8 tens + 0 ones — 51
7 tens + 3 ones — 80
5 tens + 1 one — 42

173

Place Value: Ones, Tens

Directions: Write the numbers for the tens and ones. Then, add.

Example:

2 tens + 7 ones
20 + 7
27

4 tens + 2 ones
40 + 2
42

2 tens + 4 ones
20 + 4
24

9 tens + 3 ones
90 + 3
93

6 tens + 8 ones
60 + 8
68

174

Your Total Solution for Second Grade

Answer Key

Place Value: Hundreds

The place value of a digit or numeral is shown by where it is in the number. For example, in the number **123**, **1** has the place value of **hundreds**, **2** is **tens**, and **3** is **ones**.

Directions: Study the examples. Then, write the missing numbers in the blanks.

Examples:

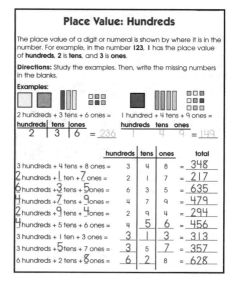

2 hundreds + 3 tens + 6 ones =

hundreds	tens	ones
2	3	6

= 236

1 hundred + 4 tens + 9 ones =

hundreds	tens	ones
1	4	9

= 149

	hundreds	tens	ones	total
3 hundreds + 4 tens + 8 ones =	3	4	8	= 348
2 hundreds + 1 ten + 7 ones =	2	1	7	= 217
6 hundreds + 3 tens + 5 ones =	6	3	5	= 635
4 hundreds + 7 tens + 9 ones =	4	7	9	= 479
2 hundreds + 9 tens + 4 ones =	2	9	4	= 294
4 hundreds + 5 tens + 6 ones =	4	5	6	= 456
3 hundreds + 1 ten + 3 ones =	3	1	3	= 313
3 hundreds + 5 tens + 7 ones =	3	5	7	= 357
6 hundreds + 2 tens + 8 ones =	6	2	8	= 628

175

Place Value: Hundreds

Directions: Write the numbers for hundreds, tens, and ones. Then, add.

Example:

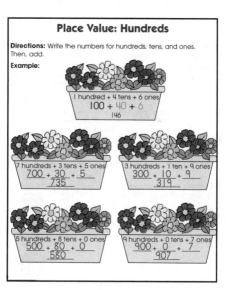

1 hundred + 4 tens + 6 ones
100 + 40 + 6
146

7 hundreds + 3 tens + 5 ones
700 + 30 + 5
735

3 hundreds + 1 ten + 9 ones
300 + 10 + 9
319

5 hundreds + 8 tens + 0 ones
500 + 80 + 0
580

9 hundreds + 0 tens + 7 ones
900 + 0 + 7
907

176

Place Value: Thousands

Directions: Study the example. Write the missing numbers.

Example:

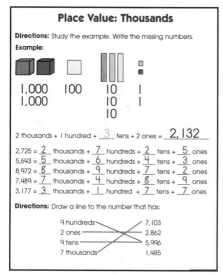

1,000   100   10   1
1,000   10   1
               10

2 thousands + 1 hundred + 3 tens + 2 ones = 2,132

2,725 = 2 thousands + 7 hundreds + 2 tens + 5 ones
5,643 = 5 thousands + 6 hundreds + 4 tens + 3 ones
8,972 = 8 thousands + 9 hundreds + 7 tens + 2 ones
7,489 = 7 thousands + 4 hundreds + 8 tens + 9 ones
3,177 = 3 thousands + 1 hundred + 7 tens + 7 ones

Directions: Draw a line to the number that has:

9 hundreds — 7,103
2 ones — 2,862
9 tens — 5,996
7 thousands — 1,485

177

Place Value: Thousands

7,621

thousands
hundreds
tens
ones

Directions: Tell which number is in each place.

Thousands place:
2,456 → 2
4,621 → 4
3,456 → 3

Tens place:
4,286 → 8
1,234 → 3
5,678 → 7

Hundreds place:
6,321 → 3
3,210 → 2
7,871 → 8

Ones place:
5,432 → 2
6,531 → 1
9,980 → 0

178

Place Value: Thousands

Directions: Use the code to color the fan.

If the answer has:
9 thousands, color it **pink**.
6 thousands, color it **green**.
5 hundreds, color it **orange**.
8 tens, color it **red**.
3 ones, color it **blue**.

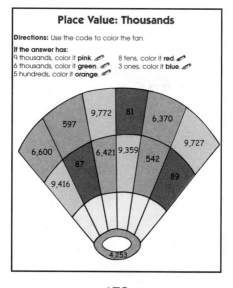

9,772   81
597   6,370
6,600   6,421 9,359   9,727
        87   542
9,416   89
4,253

179

Graphs

A **graph** is a drawing that shows information about numbers.

Directions: Count the apples in each row. Color the boxes to show how many apples have bites taken out of them.

Example:

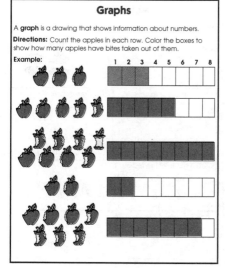

180

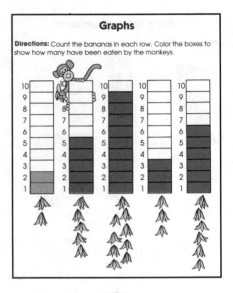

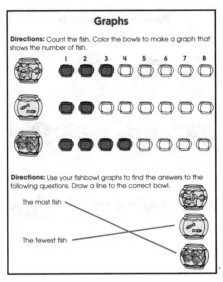

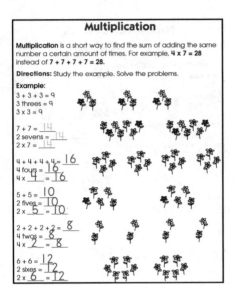

Answer Key

Graphs

Directions: Count the bananas in each row. Color the boxes to show how many have been eaten by the monkeys.

181

Graphs

Directions: Count the fish. Color the bowls to make a graph that shows the number of fish.

Directions: Use your fishbowl graphs to find the answers to the following questions. Draw a line to the correct bowl.

The most fish

The fewest fish

182

Multiplication

Multiplication is a short way to find the sum of adding the same number a certain amount of times. For example, **4 x 7 = 28** instead of **7 + 7 + 7 + 7 = 28.**

Directions: Study the example. Solve the problems.

Example:

3 + 3 + 3 = 9
3 threes = 9
3 x 3 = 9

7 + 7 = _14_
2 sevens = _14_
2 x 7 = _14_

4 + 4 + 4 + 4 = _16_
4 fours = _16_
4 x _4_ = _16_

5 + 5 = _10_
2 fives = _10_
2 x _5_ = _10_

2 + 2 + 2 + 2 = _8_
4 twos = _8_
4 x _2_ = _8_

6 + 6 = _12_
2 sixes = _12_
2 x _6_ = _12_

183

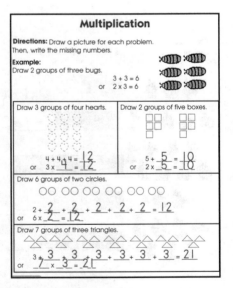

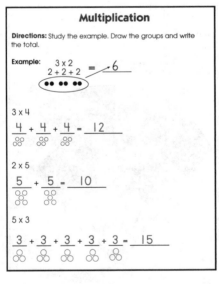

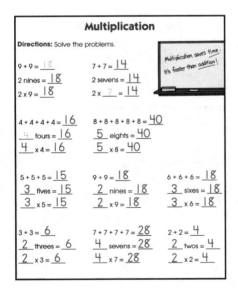

Multiplication

Directions: Draw a picture for each problem. Then, write the missing numbers.

Example:
Draw 2 groups of three bugs.

3 + 3 = 6
or 2 x 3 = 6

Draw 3 groups of four hearts. | Draw 2 groups of five boxes.

4 + 4 + 4 = _12_
or 3 x _4_ = _12_

5 + 5 = _10_
or 2 x _5_ = _10_

Draw 6 groups of two circles.

2 + _2_ + _2_ + _2_ + _2_ + 2 = _12_
or 6 x _2_ = _12_

Draw 7 groups of three triangles.

3 + _3_ + _3_ + 3 + _3_ + _3_ + 3 = _21_
or _7_ x _3_ = _21_

184

Multiplication

Directions: Study the example. Draw the groups and write the total.

Example:
3 x 2
2 + 2 + 2 = _6_

3 x 4
_4_ + _4_ + _4_ = _12_

2 x 5
_5_ + _5_ = _10_

5 x 3
_3_ + _3_ + _3_ + _3_ + _3_ = _15_

185

Multiplication

Directions: Solve the problems.

Multiplication saves time. It's faster than addition!

9 + 9 = _18_
2 nines = _18_
2 x 9 = _18_

7 + 7 = _14_
2 sevens = _14_
2 x _7_ = _14_

4 + 4 + 4 + 4 = _16_
_4_ fours = _16_
_4_ x 4 = _16_

8 + 8 + 8 + 8 + 8 = _40_
_5_ eights = _40_
_5_ x 8 = _40_

5 + 5 + 5 = _15_
_3_ fives = _15_
_3_ x 5 = _15_

9 + 9 = _18_
_2_ nines = _18_
_2_ x 9 = _18_

6 + 6 + 6 = _18_
_3_ sixes = _18_
_3_ x 6 = _18_

3 + 3 = _6_
_2_ threes = _6_
_2_ x 3 = _6_

7 + 7 + 7 + 7 = _28_
_4_ sevens = _28_
_4_ x 7 = _28_

2 + 2 = _4_
_2_ twos = _4_
_2_ x 2 = _4_

186

Your Total Solution for Second Grade

Answer Key

Problem-Solving

Directions: Tell if you add, subtract, or multiply. Then, write the answer.

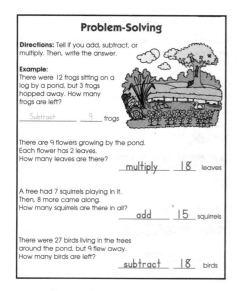

Example:
There were 12 frogs sitting on a log by a pond, but 3 frogs hopped away. How many frogs are left?

Subtract _9_ frogs

There are 9 flowers growing by the pond. Each flower has 2 leaves. How many leaves are there?

multiply _18_ leaves

A tree had 7 squirrels playing in it. Then, 8 more came along. How many squirrels are there in all?

add _15_ squirrels

There were 27 birds living in the trees around the pond, but 9 flew away. How many birds are left?

subtract _18_ birds

187

Fractions: Half, Third, Fourth

A **fraction** is a number that names part of a whole, such as $\frac{1}{2}$ or $\frac{1}{3}$

Directions: Study the examples. Color the correct fraction of each shape.

Examples:

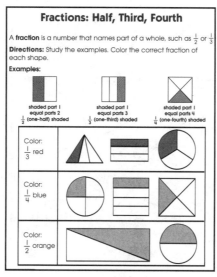

188

Fractions: Half, Third, Fourth

Directions: Study the examples. Circle the fraction that shows the shaded part. Then, circle the fraction that shows the white part.

Examples:

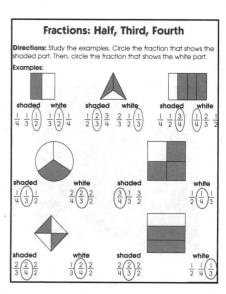

189

Fractions: Half, Third, Fourth

Directions: Draw a line from the fraction to the correct shape.

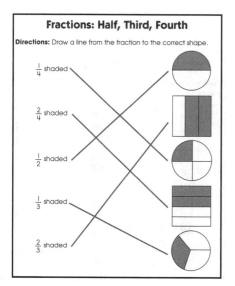

$\frac{1}{4}$ shaded

$\frac{2}{4}$ shaded

$\frac{1}{2}$ shaded

$\frac{1}{3}$ shaded

$\frac{2}{3}$ shaded

190

Problem-Solving: Fractions

Directions: Read each problem. Use the pictures to help you solve the problem. Write the fraction that answers the question.

Simon and Jessie shared a pizza. Together they ate $\frac{3}{4}$ of the pizza. How much of the pizza is left? _$\frac{1}{4}$_

Sylvia baked a cherry pie. She gave $\frac{1}{3}$ to her grandmother and $\frac{1}{3}$ to a friend. How much of the pie did she keep? _$\frac{1}{3}$_

Timmy erased $\frac{1}{2}$ of the blackboard before the bell rang for recess. How much of the blackboard does he have left to erase? _$\frac{1}{2}$_

Directions: Read the problem. Draw your own picture to help you solve the problem. Write the fraction that answers the question.

Sarah mowed $\frac{1}{4}$ of the yard before lunch. How much does she have left to mow? _$\frac{3}{4}$_

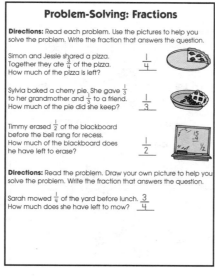

191

Geometry

Geometry is mathematics that has to do with lines and shapes.

Directions: Color the shapes.

Color the triangles **blue**.
Color the circles **red**.
Color the squares **green**.
Color the rectangles **pink**.

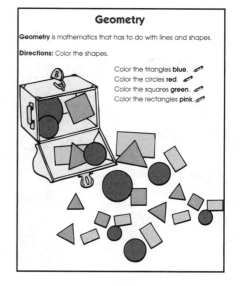

192

Answer Key

Geometry

Directions: Cut out the tangram below. Mix up the pieces. Try to put it back together into a square.

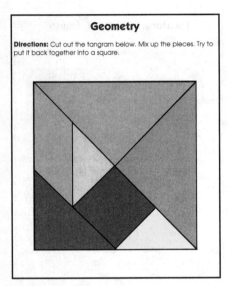

193

Geometry

Directions: Draw a line from the word to the shape.

Use a red line for circles. Use a yellow line for rectangles.
Use a blue line for squares. Use a green line for triangles.

Circle   Square   Triangle   Rectangle

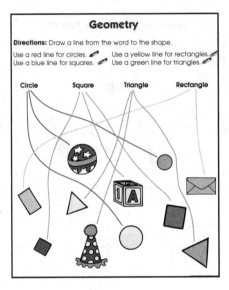

195

Measurement: Inches

An **inch** is a unit of length in the standard measurement system.

Directions: Use a ruler to measure each object to the nearest inch.

1 inch

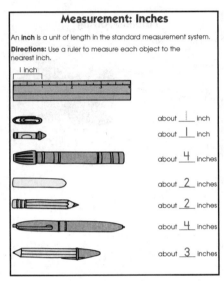

about __1__ inch
about __1__ inch
about __4__ inches
about __2__ inches
about __2__ inches
about __4__ inches
about __3__ inches

196

Measurement

Directions: Cut out the ruler. Measure each object to the nearest inch.

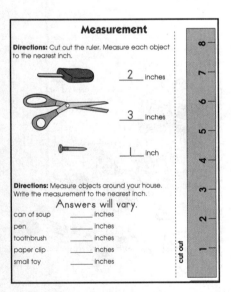

__2__ inches
__3__ inches
__1__ inch

Directions: Measure objects around your house. Write the measurement to the nearest inch.

Answers will vary.

can of soup	_____ inches
pen	_____ inches
toothbrush	_____ inches
paper clip	_____ inches
small toy	_____ inches

197

Measurement

Directions: Use the ruler to measure the fish to the nearest inch.

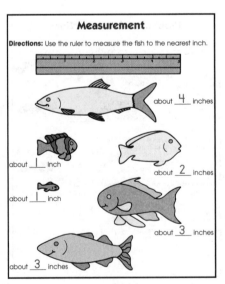

about __4__ inches
about __1__ inch
about __2__ inches
about __1__ inch
about __3__ inches
about __3__ inches

199

Measurement: Centimeters

A **centimeter** is a unit of length in the metric system. There are 2.54 centimeters in an inch.

Directions: Use a centimeter ruler to measure the crayons to the nearest centimeter.

Example: The first crayon is about 7 centimeters long.

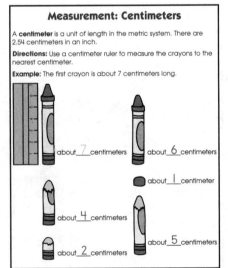

about __7__ centimeters   about __6__ centimeters
about __1__ centimeter
about __4__ centimeters   about __5__ centimeters
about __2__ centimeters

200

Your Total Solution for Second Grade

Answer Key

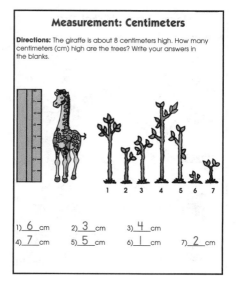

Measurement: Centimeters

Directions: The giraffe is about 8 centimeters high. How many centimeters (cm) high are the trees? Write your answers in the blanks.

1) _6_ cm   2) _3_ cm   3) _4_ cm
4) _7_ cm   5) _5_ cm   6) _1_ cm   7) _2_ cm

201

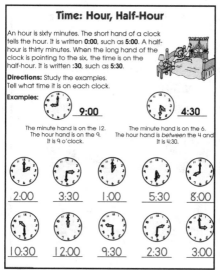

Time: Hour, Half-Hour

An hour is sixty minutes. The short hand of a clock tells the hour. It is written **0:00**, such as **5:00**. A half-hour is thirty minutes. When the long hand of the clock is pointing to the six, the time is on the half-hour. It is written **:30**, such as **5:30**.

Directions: Study the examples. Tell what time it is on each clock.

Examples:

9:00
The minute hand is on the 12. The hour hand is on the 9. It is 9 o'clock.

4:30
The minute hand is on the 6. The hour hand is *between* the 4 and It is 4:30.

2:00   3:30   1:00   5:30   8:00

10:30   12:00   9:30   2:30   3:00

202

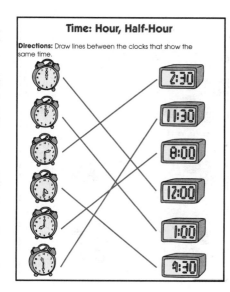

Time: Hour, Half-Hour

Directions: Draw lines between the clocks that show the same time.

2:30
11:30
8:00
12:00
1:00
4:30

203

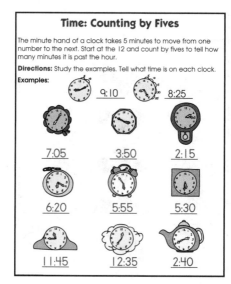

Time: Counting by Fives

The minute hand of a clock takes 5 minutes to move from one number to the next. Start at the 12 and count by fives to tell how many minutes it is past the hour.

Directions: Study the examples. Tell what time it is on each clock.

Examples:

9:10   8:25

7:05   3:50   2:15

6:20   5:55   5:30

11:45   12:35   2:40

204

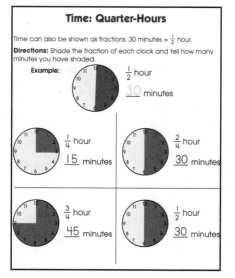

Time: Quarter-Hours

Time can also be shown as fractions. 30 minutes = $\frac{1}{2}$ hour.

Directions: Shade the fraction of each clock and tell how many minutes you have shaded.

Example:

$\frac{1}{2}$ hour
_30_ minutes

$\frac{1}{4}$ hour
_15_ minutes

$\frac{2}{4}$ hour
_30_ minutes

$\frac{3}{4}$ hour
_45_ minutes

$\frac{1}{2}$ hour
_30_ minutes

205

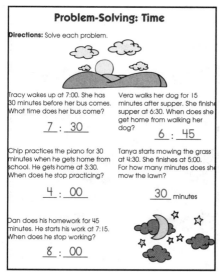

Problem-Solving: Time

Directions: Solve each problem.

Tracy wakes up at 7:00. She has 30 minutes before her bus comes. What time does her bus come?

_7_ : _30_

Vera walks her dog for 15 minutes after supper. She finishes supper at 6:30. When does she get home from walking her dog?

_6_ : _45_

Chip practices the piano for 30 minutes when he gets home from school. He gets home at 3:30. When does he stop practicing?

_4_ : _00_

Tanya starts mowing the grass at 4:30. She finishes at 5:00. For how many minutes does she mow the lawn?

_30_ minutes

Dan does his homework for 45 minutes. He starts his work at 7:15. When does he stop working?

_8_ : _00_

206

Answer Key

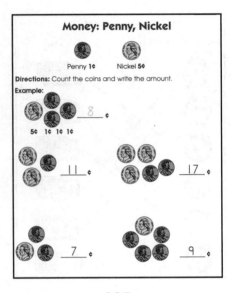

Money: Penny, Nickel

Penny 1¢   Nickel 5¢

Directions: Count the coins and write the amount.

Example:

__8__ ¢

5¢ 1¢ 1¢ 1¢

__11__ ¢

__17__ ¢

__7__ ¢

__9__ ¢

207

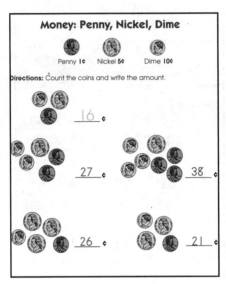

Money: Penny, Nickel, Dime

Penny 1¢   Nickel 5¢   Dime 10¢

Directions: Count the coins and write the amount.

__16__ ¢

__27__ ¢

__38__ ¢

__26__ ¢

__21__ ¢

208

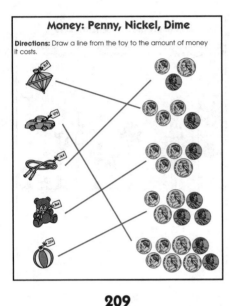

Money: Penny, Nickel, Dime

Directions: Draw a line from the toy to the amount of money it costs.

209

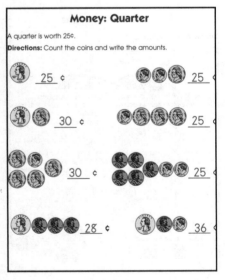

Money: Quarter

A quarter is worth 25¢.

Directions: Count the coins and write the amounts.

__25__ ¢   __25__ ¢

__30__ ¢   __25__ ¢

__30__ ¢   __25__ ¢

__28__ ¢   __36__ ¢

210

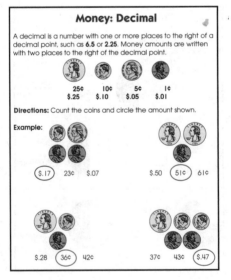

Money: Decimal

A decimal is a number with one or more places to the right of a decimal point, such as **6.5** or **2.25**. Money amounts are written with two places to the right of the decimal point.

25¢   10¢   5¢   1¢
$.25 $.10 $.05 $.01

Directions: Count the coins and circle the amount shown.

Example:

(\$.17)   23¢   \$.07   \$.50   (51¢)   61¢

\$.28   (36¢)   42¢   37¢   43¢   (\$.47)

211

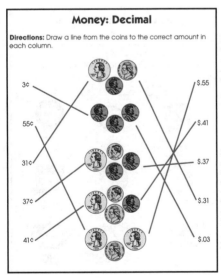

Money: Decimal

Directions: Draw a line from the coins to the correct amount in each column.

3¢   \$.55

55¢   \$.41

31¢   \$.37

37¢   \$.31

41¢   \$.03

212

Your Total Solution for Second Grade

Answer Key

Money: Dollar

One dollar equals 100 cents. It is written **$1.00**.

Directions: Count the money and write the amounts.

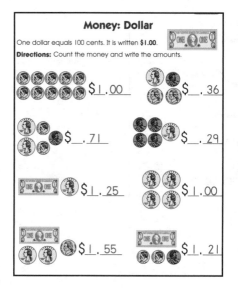

$1.00 $ .36

$ .71 $ .29

$1.25 $1.00

$1.55 $1.21

213

Adding Money

Directions: Write the amount of money using decimals. Then, add to find the total amount.

Example:
$1.00
.05
+ .02
$1.07

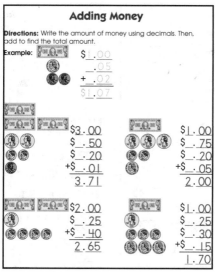

$3.00
$ .50
$ .20
+$ .01
3.71

$1.00
$ .75
$ .20
+$ .05
2.00

$2.00
$ .25
+$ .40
2.65

$1.00
$ .25
$ .30
+$ .15
1.70

214

Money: Practice

Directions: Draw a line from each food item to the correct amount of money.

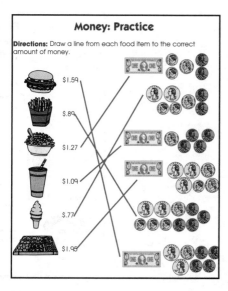

$1.59

$.89

$1.27

$1.09

$.77

$1.95

215

Review

Directions: Add the money and write the total.

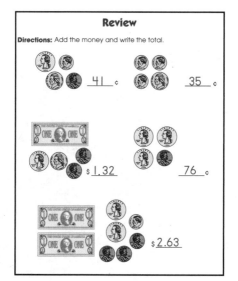

41 ¢   35 ¢

$1.32   76 ¢

$2.63

216

Problem-Solving: Money

Directions: Read each problem. Use the pictures to help you solve the problems.

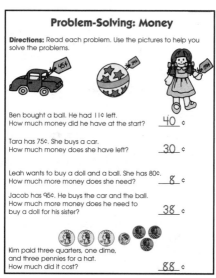

Ben bought a ball. He had 11¢ left.
How much money did he have at the start?   40 ¢

Tara has 75¢. She buys a car.
How much money does she have left?   30 ¢

Leah wants to buy a doll and a ball. She has 80¢.
How much more money does she need?   8 ¢

Jacob has 95¢. He buys the car and the ball.
How much more money does he need to
buy a doll for his sister?   38 ¢

Kim paid three quarters, one dime,
and three pennies for a hat.
How much did it cost?   88 ¢

217

Review

Two-Digit Addition and Subtraction

Directions: Add or subtract using regrouping, if needed.

66 − 37 = 29	38 + 18 = 56	87 − 69 = 18	52 − 15 = 37	40 + 17 = 57
84 + 17 = 101	65 + 14 = 79	99 − 48 = 51	61 − 36 = 25	56 + 46 = 102

Place Value: Hundreds and Thousands

Directions: Draw a line to the correct number.

4 hundreds + 3 tens + 2 ones — 7,201

6 hundreds + 7 tens + 6 ones — 290

5 thousands + 3 hundreds + 7 tens + 2 ones — 432

2 hundreds + 9 tens + 0 ones — 676

7 thousands + 2 hundreds + 0 tens + 1 one — 5,372

Three-Digit Addition and Subtraction

Directions: Add or subtract, remembering to regroup, if needed.

458 − 248 = 210	793 − 414 = 379	822 − 460 = 362	528 + 319 = 847	697 + 108 = 805	569 + 288 = 857

218

Answer Key

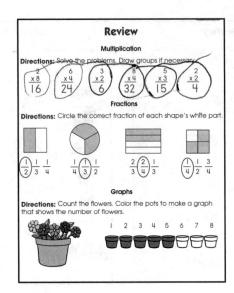

219

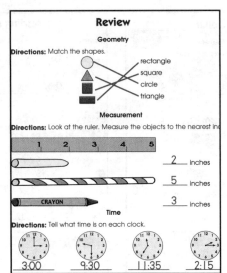

220

Your Total Solution for Second Grade